Ritual Journeys
with
Great British Goddesses

Discover thirteen British Goddesses,
worshipped in pre-Roman Britain,
create rituals, and journey through meditation for your
spiritual development and growth

Susie Fox

ISBN: 978-1-4669-4652-1 (sc)
ISBN: 978-1-4669-4654-5 (hc)
ISBN: 978-1-4669-4653-8 (e)

Library of Congress Control Number: 2012912772

Trafford rev. 04/28/2015

 www.trafford.com

North America & international
toll-free: 1 888 232 4444 (USA & Canada)
fax: 812 355 4082

To Nisey
my closest friend

Acknowledgements

Ellie Dobson, for her inspiring Goddess ways, and an unforgettable trip to Glastonbury. Joseph Dobson for setting up my computer, lap top and endless patience and forbearance with all things technical. Jeremy Dobson, for providing discussion and insight. Alice Firminger, who exemplifies a woman of strength and determination. Will Firminger, for revealing how healthy cynicism creates balance. Jack Firminger, for accompanying me on many visits to ancient sites. Nisey O'Donnell for proof reading and positive criticism. The Kith of the Earthen Star, a marvellous, witty, creative, daring, interesting, unusual, understanding, loving, caring, healing, outrageous, mad, bad and downright dangerous group!

Contents

Preface

I have written Ritual Journeys with Great British Goddesses to answer the question: Who are the *British* Goddesses that can be worshipped in the 21ˢᵗ Century?

There is a hunger in the 21ˢᵗ century to connect with the Divine Feminine, and when people walk their spiritual path and explore the concept of The Goddess or Divine Feminine, they find Goddesses from all over the world presented attractively, with detailed mythology, supported by stories, meditations, oracle sets, tarot cards and illustrations that enable them to connect to feminine spirituality. Yet there is very little for those of us who have British roots or an interest in Britain's indigenous spirituality, and would like to explore spirituality through the concept of the British Divine Feminine.

There is a reliance on medieval written texts, such as The Mabinogian, and the Arthurian Legends that originated with Geoffrey of Monmouth's writings in the 12ᵗʰ Century and that enjoyed a resurgence in 19ᵗʰ century romanticism, to provide us with the names of British Goddesses. From these sources we explore Goddesses such as Cerridwen, Bridget, Rhiannon, The Morrigan, Guinevere and Morgan le Fay. However, the history of these Goddesses is not rooted in ancient times, although it may be argued that these stories are the written version of an aural tradition that goes back thousands of years.

I have researched British Goddesses who were worshipped in Britain prior to the invasion of the Romans. They have been discovered through archaeological finds, or documented by Roman inscriptions. Those who are already interested in Goddess worship can explore the Goddesses in this book, knowing that they have ancient British roots and are indigenous to the British Isles.

Ritual Journeys with Great British Goddesses provides thirteen rituals that are comprehensive and easy to use, adaptable, and focus on areas of need and development that are common to women and men. The rituals also link to the ancient British festivals, Samhain, Imbolc, Beltane, and Lughnasadh, as well as the Winter and Summer Solstices and the Spring and Autumn Equinoxes. It is a book for active engagement with the Goddesses.

Unlike many books of rituals, Ritual Journeys with Great British Goddesses provides history and a location, so that the reader will be able to learn about the Goddess and about the area of Britain in which she was located. I have walked the land local to each Goddess and used the concept of the land to support the ritual. I want to give the reader an appetite for exploring Britain in pilgrimage and a sense of ownership of the rituals that will lead to a greater depth of spirituality, understanding and wisdom.

The rituals in this book are focussed on calling in the Goddess. However, it is acknowledged that the balance of female and male is necessary, and you are free to call in a god of your choice, or a masculine spiritual being. It is also acknowledged that each woman and goddess carries a masculine aspect to balance their femininity.

Introduction to the Goddess

Ritual Journeys with Great British Goddesses provides a variety of rituals, that take us on a journey through the year, and invokes a Goddess during each ritual who will bring us to a place of growth and change.

There are many cultures in the world that acknowledge the presence of the Goddess and have rich traditions of myth and legend. Thriving Goddess worship can be found in many countries. But whilst there are many written records of stories concerning Welsh, Scottish and Irish Goddesses, there is far less recorded information about English Goddesses. Seeking Celtic Goddesses is not difficult, until the origin of the Goddess is uncovered and we find her worshipped in Greece, France, Germany, or Scandinavia. Many Goddesses can be traced back to Italy, and travelled with the Roman invaders to Britain.

The investigation to discover indigenous British Goddesses led to a point in time that was pre-Roman invasion, and documented by the Romans during the years of invasion during which they adopted local Gods and Goddesses, or wrote about the society and culture met in Britain. Although loosely referred to as "Celtic", this era is also known as The Iron Age.

The word "Keltoi" (Greek: Κελτοί) was used by Hecateaus of Miletus in BCE 517 when describing the European tribes of Iron Age farmers and traders as they migrated across Europe, eventually settling in the British Isles. It was from the Greek "Keltoi", that the word "Celt" developed. The Romans however, who invaded Britain in BC55/54[1], and later in AD43[2], preferred to use the word Galli[3] referred to now as "Gaul".

The concept of the "Celt" has been mythologized by the romantic writers of the 19th century, until the word has become commonly associated with the stories and legends, and Gods and Goddesses, of some fuzzy far-off-in-the-mists-of-time era when dragons abounded and were slain by knights in shining armour, fair maidens were captured and rescued, and great deeds were done.

However, although the indigenous population of Britain (the Brythons) would never have referred to themselves as Celts, it is the Goddesses of these people that we are going to meditate on, learn about, and invoke in our rituals.

So who are these Sacred Ladies?

The first Goddess that humans acknowledged was the Mother Goddess, a fertility deity on whom the survival of humans depended. Examples of images have been found from as early as 10,000 BC. It was understood that the same primary energy granted fertility to the land, and created the birth of a child. Both ensured the human race continued. The archetype of the "Mother" was personified, and deified.

These ancestors were the hunter-gatherers, a pre-agrarian society of subsistence foragers who tracked the animals they killed for food, and who were drawn to sources of water, as this was where the animals gathered. The "Mother", and the springs, rivers and lakes, were connected as a source of life. The local springs, rivers and lakes were worshipped, first in themselves, then personified and worshipped as a local deity.

The Moon symbolises the very same pattern of birth, growth, fullness, decay and disappearance as both the course of life, and the course of pregnancy. The moon is then reborn, and, our ancestors say, so are we.

---

[1]   Julius Caesar
[2]   Aulus Plautius, sent by the Roman Emperor Claudius I
[3]   Possibly meaning "strength"

The concept of the Goddess gradually changed from being the "Mother", to being three-in-one: the Maiden, the Mother, and the Crone. The Crone dies and is reborn again as the Maiden. As farming methods became more pastoral and arable, the Goddess with her triple aspects was connected to the seasons of the year. The Maiden is worshipped in Spring, conceives a child at the Spring Equinox, becomes the heavily pregnant Great Mother by late Summer, and gives birth to her son at the Winter Solstice. The Crone is worshipped in the Autumn, when the sunlight fills fewer hours each day, and the darkness encroaches.

We will utilize this concept in our rituals, as we have the benefit of knowledge that our Iron Age ancestors did not have. For the Iron Age worshippers, the triplicity of the Goddess was not Maiden—Mother—Crone. Triplicity was a way of empowering the Goddess in a visual way, well understood by the Iron Age worshipper. One of the carved panels found at Coventina's Well at Carrawborough, by Hadrian's Wall, had three nymphs carved onto it. This does not show three different nymphs, but a triple Coventina, and the person who made it was empowering her three times.

The Goddess did not stand alone however, nor were men neglected. The God took the part of consort to the Goddess. He is born at Winter Solstice, grows to a young man by February (Imbolc). He fathers the next God at the Spring Equinox or Beltane, and is killed at the Summer Solstice. After this, the dark encroaches over the land, he passes into the Underworld at Samhain, and stays there until the Winter Solstice when he is born again, bringing with him increasing light. The male deity has taken the form of Cernunnos the Hunter, the Green Man, and the Sun God. Variations abound, especially with the time of the conception of The next God which may be the Spring Equinox on 21st March, "Lady Day" on 25th March, or Beltane, 1st of May.

When the Mesolithic tribesmen set off on their hunting expedition, a chosen tribesman dressed up in skins and placed antlers on his head taken from the last kill. The hunt was acted out, and given a very satisfactory conclusion. This was an example of sympathetic magic to ensure the success of the kill. The deity of Cernunuos takes the same form, of a hunter with antlers, as represented in iconography on the Gundestrup Cauldron.

The Sun was personified by both the male and the female, with the Norse Goddess Sol giving her name to the British Sunday. Sol, also known as Sunna, Sunne and Frau Sunne (Germanic), drove her chariot across the skies, pulled by her horses Arvak and Alsuid. The chariot bore the sun, and was chased by the wolf, Skill, whose intention was to devour her.

The Green Man's icon is found on many church portals throughout Britain. There are also examples of Green Women as well, but they are far fewer. His face, sprouting foliage and oak leaves, communicates the importance of the cycle of the year, and the fertility of the land.

So how "British" are our British Goddesses? We have a record of many local deities due to the historical writings of the Roman historians, and the Roman inscriptions and panel carvings found at their sacred temples. The Romans gave Latin names to the local deities, and it is sometimes hard to find the original Brythonic names. Some deities' names appear only once, whilst others have associated information. For instance, Andred seems to be the same Goddess as the Romanised Goddess, Andraste. Sul may have been spelt Suil in Old Irish, meaning "eye" or "gap". Was this Goddess named after the "orifice" from which the healing waters ran? In the Proto-Celtic language, she was Su-Lijis, the "Good Flooding One". However, the Romans adopted her as Sulis, and then assimilated her into their own pantheon of deities, where she became Sulis-Minerva. Sul may be a derivative of the word Sol, and worshipped as the Sun Goddess. Some of the Goddesses chosen for this book have Romanised names as that is our only record.

The Brythons rarely used theonyms of a personal nature for their deities. Rigantona stems from "Rigani" meaning Queen, "on" refers to deities, as in Matrona, Epona, or Sirona and the suffix "a" constitutes a feminine ending. Deities who were personally named carried the name of a local river, or sacred spring, rather than a woman or man's name. Grouped deities such as the Dervonnae (spirits of the Oak), or the Niskaie (Water Sprites) were more common.

As arable farming developed, the Iron Age tribes needed more land, and they migrated, along with their deities and sacred practices, throughout Europe and to Britain. Trade routes were established, and these brought traders from many parts of the world to Britain's shores. And so the "British" Goddesses were often very well travelled and known under different or similar names as far a-field as Greece. Elen of the Ways may have started her journey in Greece as Helen of Troy. Epona, the Horse Goddess, so widely invoked in Britain, was Gallo-Roman in origin. Rosmerta arrived from Gaul, and Habondia, her worship peaking in the medieval era, may be linked to the Roman Goddess of abundance and fertility, Abundantia.

England did not exist, as such, but was part of the greater whole. The Romans named the South of England and Wales "Higher Britannia" and the Northern part of England and Scotland "Lower Britannia". It was during the Anglo Saxon and Gaullish raids, post Roman occupation, that the Brythons in "England" retreated into "Wales", "Scotland", and "Cornwall" taking protection from the highlands and using established hill forts. During this time, whilst the mythologies of these places flourished, "England's" cultural heritage was lost to the invaders. The rise of Christianity completed the process.

So, intuitively, along with our historical knowledge, we will draw the essence of the Goddess from nature, the pools, springs, lakes, streams and rivers, trees and rocks, the sun and the moon, and from our own hearts.

Creative Transformation and the Art of Ritual

Ritual is a means of human expression, communication and a vehicle for development and change.

From the moment of birth onwards, women and men are destined to grow, develop, and transform. This process can be positive, or negative, but change will happen, either way. It is said, "You cannot change a person," and the new bride is warned, "He'll never change, you know!" when she has her last minute doubts. Likewise, "She is very set in her ways!" But people do change; they have to. Life and living enforce it, like it or not! And often the case is that they do not like it one little bit. Creative Ritual can make this process exciting and fun, or at least, smooth out the way.

Learning new skills, expanding physical, emotional, mental and spiritual awareness, and embracing new possibilities, are challenges that can be met as opportunities for growth and maturity, or as conflicting difficulties to be fought against. Through the multitude of experiences that life brings us, we have lessons to learn, obstacles to overcome, grief to bear, joy to celebrate, new friends to love, and established friends to say goodbye to. If we are open to this process, we become broader in outlook, and deeper in personality.

Some folk resist change with all their might. This does not mean that change does not happen. "If you are not moving forwards, you are slipping back." If resisted the changes may happen more slowly, but sometimes, instead of positive growth, the result is backtracking. People exchange the opportunity to expand their horizons, for the "safer" option of narrowing their vision, blinkered by habits that become, in effect, a prison. So, they develop into a person who lives and copes with life in that fashion, changing their outlook to within ever narrower confinements.

Ritual is about embracing change, transformation, development and openness to experience. It is about surrendering to life's energy and using the momentum of experience to propel oneself forwards.

Ritual enables us to express difficulties, give thanks, show enthusiasm, and bless the challenge of new opportunities with encouragement. It helps us face transformation bravely.

It also raises questions, such as, Do you believe in God? How many countless times has this been asked, and answered, or ignored. What is your answer? He, She, Son, Daughter, Adult, Baby, Divine Spirit, the Son that died and rose again, the Matriarch, Good Man or Good Woman, Prophet, Elemental, Deva, Angel, Monad, one God, one Goddess, many Gods, many Goddesses.

Ritual enables those who believe in the spiritual expression of life, to communicate with faith that their communications will be heard, and acted upon by a Divine entity.

Thought is the starting place, followed by intention. What follows next is expressed by as many means of creativity as there are people on the planet, and then some. Most of us communicate in more than one way: speech is only one method. Try writing, drawing, painting, computer graphics, ceramics, mosaic, collage, gardening, baking, sewing, dancing, drumming . . . . the list goes on. Ritual provides the ideal place for that communication to take place.

Not only do we communicate outwardly to "Spirit", but we communicate inwardly to "Self". Who will you be communicating with? This is your journey of learning. Only you can answer this question for yourself. You may have a very clear fixed concept, a relationship, and a sturdy faith. But we change! It would be expected that your belief at this very moment is not exactly as it was five, ten, twenty or fifty years ago, any more than your understanding of your parent, or your child, sister, or work colleague is the same as it was five, ten, twenty or more years ago.

The Goddesses who are called upon during the rituals in this book were worshipped during pre-Roman times by communities of Iron Age tribes. They were important in that day, within those tribes, in their local geographical area, with their traditions, beliefs, and rituals. But for the most part the Goddesses have not got fantastical myths and legends attached to their names. During our rituals we are challenged by the following questions: is each Goddess a Goddess in her own right? Or is she a "face" or "aspect" of the Great Goddess? Is she a "Spirit?" Or is she an archetype of the greater human unconscious understanding that is recognised by all humanity? Do we worship her, or do we work alongside the Goddess—or both? Will she communicate back to us? If she does, will we understand her? How will you communicate? How the dialogue between Spirit and human evolves, is part of the adventure. Exploring these questions is part of our reason for creating ritual.

As a human creates, so expression and communication flow through them. Having created, some aspect of life is different—even if it is simply that the seeds that were in the packet, are now filled with your ritual intention, sprinkled on compost, and watered. An event has taken place. Because we have done a practical activity on the physical level, we can remember it, and refer back to it when needed. This is important especially when coping with a difficulty or for healing. It is also enjoyably satisfying to have memories of celebrations and thanks giving.

Enjoyment is a very large part of ritual. Whilst not every ritual is a thanksgiving or celebration, many are very joyful times. Grief and sorrow are part of life, but even when these are the focus of the ritual, we can finish feeling a satisfaction and deep peace.

Ritual provides a safe place, a well-structured place, and a sacred place for our physical, emotional, mental and spiritual journey.

When should we hold a ritual? There are many reasons to hold a ritual, but one main reason is simply for enjoyment. Joyously holding a ritual to celebrate a positive outcome of a former ritual, giving thanks for the goodness in life, dedicating and blessing a new project and marking the passage from one state of development to another; these are all positive reasons to hold a ritual.

Very often people are provoked to hold a ritual to help them through a difficult time. It is a way of dealing with the grief, loss, pain, and anguish they feel. Sometimes a ritual is held to speed healing. Festivals are often community or family celebrations, rather than solitary events. But even if you are having a major family celebration, you may wish to hold your own solitary ritual as well. Ritual can also become part of the daily routine. A short ritual held in the morning or last thing at night before going to bed will help a person connect to the Divine and help support a clearer direction.

There are no fixed rules when creating your own ritual. For the rituals in this book, I have suggested using items, locations, and times that are intended to support the intention of the ritual. You can substitute items depending on what you already own, or what you can find locally. Your intuition will let you know if substitutions are supportive, or if they detract from the intention of the ritual. The main aim is to have a go, and use the rituals in this book as a template for your own creative ideas. If you cannot use a suggested location then maybe you can bring part of the location to your own home. Some people will live near the sea, and can use the sea shore without problem. Others may wish to use a collection of seashells to decorate their ritual space.

Simplicity is the key to a powerful ritual. Keep your symbolism, intention, and supporting activities to the point. Trying to hit ten bulls' eyes with one ritual arrow will diffuse the power of the ritual. One arrow will hit one mark, and you need the focus, intention and energy to manifest it.

Self————➤Arrow of Intention————➤Target

Mental and emotional distractions do not help. Try to keep your mental and emotional state in line with the focus of your ritual.

Thought—→Intention—→Build Energy—→Release Energy—→Result

Our emotions are rarely stable, but acknowledging them and working with ourselves as we are at the given time is one way forward. Putting off the ritual until we are in the mood may mean that we miss the window of opportunity. However, if we are overtired, poorly, angry or upset, then trying to hold a ritual may not be conducive. So use common sense and decide if you can hold your planned ritual at the time and in the place you planned it, or whether flexibility and adaptability is needed.

Preparing spiritually is also important. It is likely that we will clear a space physically for the ritual to take place. As we clear the physical space we can also clear the energy field as well. The besom broomstick was used historically for both physical space cleansing and energy cleaning too. Brush a clean broom through the space with the intention of clearing negative energy away. Or, having vacuumed and tidied, open the windows and use a smudge stick of white sage to waft round the room. Basil essential oil dropped onto water in a diffuser is very cleansing, and Frankincense joss sticks are excellent. There are many ways to clear space but those three methods work well.

For cleansing the human aura a smouldering smudge stick can be wafted around the body. Concentrate on cleansing and hold a strong intention that the negative energy will leave. A purification bath using two tablespoons of sea or rock salt in the water cleanses the aura and refreshes the body.

What you wear is your own choice. Some may not want to wear clothes at all. One idea is to have a pendant, a piece of jewellery, or a particular outfit that you use each time you hold a ritual. That in itself becomes symbolic and marks the change from the mundane to the special.

Creating atmosphere is important and part of the creative process. Consider what lifts you out of ordinary life and helps you to enter a place that is neither of this time, nor of this world. We are not trying to force a false situation. This is about enabling, enjoying, and supporting the truth of our ritual. It is about making a special time and a special place in the midst of the normal and usual. This helps us focus on our intentions, and open our minds to hear that still, small voice. It is also honouring to the Goddess.

If our child has a birthday party, and friends are invited, then we dress up, make a special cake, light candles, play music, and tie up balloons. What we are aiming for in creating an atmosphere in ritual is not dissimilar to creating a party atmosphere to ensure the party is special and different from every day tea. Having suitable ambient music playing, incense burning, special clothes, jewellery, tools, and decorations are all part of the ritual. But, as always, do not get over burdened. One candle and a meditation is a ritual in itself. Meditation may come easier if there is a candle, or some incense or a little music in the background. Even in the most basic and short rituals, it helps to create a special environment.

What can we do outside? This is harder. We take portable candles and the wind blows them out. We take incense and it is lost in the air. We take circle marker stones, and wonder where on the pebbly beach they went to. Then it rains!

What did our Bronze Age ancestors do? They created stone circles and lit a fire. Apart from that we know little, other than the evidence left by burial rites. But we can learn those simple lessons. Make a boundary and place a symbol for each element within it. After that we are left with the wind, air, rain, soil, stones, trees and flowers. Candles can be used, but need to be housed in lanterns. Water can be contained by bowls and cups. Incense sticks for outdoors can be sourced and bought. A cairn of stones and rocks may be more symbolic out of doors than transporting your crystal collection. Use natural and local elemental material, found on the chosen space rather than artificially making something from imported gear.

Spend time carefully choosing your location. It is noticeable that the Bronze Age worshippers chose naturally circular geographic landscapes in which to build their stone circles. Standing in the centre of the circle, the land forms draw close and wrap around the circle, as if trying to take part. Look for clearings, rock formations, tree edge areas that give privacy from passers by, and protection from the wind. Then welcome the trees and flowers, rocks and stones, and all the abundance of nature to join in.

Festivals and Seasons

It is hard to know exactly when rituals and celebrations would have been held in Iron Age communities, or what they comprised. The first ceremonial centres date back to 3500 BC. Archaeological evidence suggests some hill forts were built for ceremonial purposes only. These were built initially in 800-700 BC and became a dominant feature of the landscape by 500-100 BC[4].

The ceremonies corresponded to the farming year, and came into being after the nomadic hunter-gatherer tribes settled down on areas of land that they cultivated into arable and pastoral farmland. The seasons of the year and the weather became extremely important to the survival of the tribe, as the Celtic people became ever more dependent on the growth of crops and the successful breeding of livestock.

The Geni Loci, the functional and tribal Gods and Goddesses, were invoked to bless the fertility of the land and the animals, encourage successful crop growth, abundant harvests and promote survival throughout the harsh Winter months. In Celtic times, dark always preceded light and Winter preceded Summer. Therefore the New Year started at the beginning of the dark season, at Samhain.

---

[4]   Litton (1997)

CELTIC FESTIVALS

The Coligny calendar dates back to 1st Century BC[5] and shows clearly the two ceremonial times of Samhain and Lughnasadh, while suggesting these festivals were held every five years. The Coligny calendar shows that the passage of time was measured, marked and important to people during this era in Europe.

In the Iron Ages people would rise and work by the light of the sun. They also recognised the thirteen full moons of the year. Having exchanged their nomadic way of life for pastoral and arable farming, they were driven by the seasons of the year, the birth and maturing of animals, and the crop harvests.

People were expected to interact with the Gods and Goddesses to influence the weather, the fertility of the land, and the safety of the animals and crops on it. Doing nothing would lead to disaster, so rituals and festivals implementing sympathetic magic were held. No doubt these were held according the season changes and weather, rather than being bound by the modern reliance on calendars and clocks.

These days we are ashamed to miss Beltane on the 1st of May, 12 noon precisely! But no doubt the Iron Age community invoked the sun and celebrated fertility when the hawthorn bloomed, rather than on an actual date. Although the Calendar of Coligny provides evidence of a clear knowledge of the concept of time, time passing and seasonal variation, whether local peasants could access this information was another matter.

THE FIRE FESTIVALS

Samhain	31st October-1st November
Imbolc	1st-2nd February
Beltane	30th April-1st May
Lughnasadh	31st July-1st August

---

[5] Cunliffe (1999)

SAMHAIN

Samhain is also known as The Third Harvest, or The Harvest of Souls. It is held at the end of October and beginning of November, starting at sunset on 31st October and ending at sunset on 1st November. This was overlaid by the Christian Church's All Hallows Day, held on 1st November and the evening prior to this celebration became known as Hallowe'en (All Hallows Eve).

Samhain is a time when the veil between the physical world and the afterlife or spiritual world becomes very thin, and the spirits of the ancestors walk abroad. This led to traditions such as the pumpkin heads that are hollowed out to house a candle which shines through the cut out face to scare off evil spirits that are roaming around.

It is also a time of pondering on death and dying, the transitions of life, journeys and changes, the purpose and role of our blood ancestors and the influences they have had (and still may have) upon us.

For some, Samhain may be a time of thanksgiving for wonderful grandparents who have passed away. For others, they may need to free themselves from outdated thought processes that bind them to a parental or grand-parental influence that still keeps them bound. During Samhain the Crone Goddess, who holds the wisdom of old age, is especially revered and respected. The Crone passes down her knowledge to younger generations to teach them her arts.

Celebrate with branches and berries, golden leaves, pumpkins and apples. Warm punches, fruit drinks, and spiced cider are welcome. Eat gingerbread and parkin, and dried fruit and nuts. Savour deep red wine, light fires and candles for warmth and to banish the darkness.

IMBOLC

Imbolc may be derived from the Proto-Celtic word "Eumelc" meaning "first milking". It is a festival held at the very end of the Winter, when the first traces of the new Spring are showing, and the first lambing of the ewes begins. In Bronze and Iron Age periods, the climate was similar to today's Mediterranean climate. This explains why the ewes gave birth to lambs so early and were put out on the higher hills to graze as early as February 2nd.

The festival is traditionally held on the 2nd February, and heralds new beginnings, the start of the fertile growing season of the year. It is a time when the earth begins to stir and push forth new life. Today we see snowdrops and aconites peeping through frost and snow, pointing the way to the warmer months ahead.

Celebrate Imbolc with colours of white for purity, and green for new growth. Light candles to symbolise and bring forth the sun. Meditate on the pure, young, maiden Goddess. Here we find her as a young child-woman, unmarried and virginal, innocent and naive. Collect snowdrops for the altar and use white and green crystals on a white cloth. Pour a glass of milk as a libation for the Goddess. Why not use sheep's milk? Now is an excellent time to start new projects that have been considered and dreamt about during the Winter months, and ask the Goddess' blessing on them. Collect your ideas together and plan how you will action them over the rest of the year.

BELTANE

Beltane is held six months later than Samhain, at the opposite side of the wheel of the year. As with Samhain, it is a time when the veil between this world and the otherworld is thought to be thin. However, the light hours are increasing and the Winter is over, so there is less to be fearful about. Beltane was considered to be the start of Summer and was held at the beginning of May.

The cattle were sent out to the Summer pastures after wintering in the lowlands. To purify them, and increase their chances of health, two bonfires were built, and the cows were driven between them. The smoke killed the ticks and mites that accumulated through the Winter season. After driving through the cattle, couples who wished to conceive a child jumped over the fires, and when they died down the embers were taken home. In Scotland, it was traditional for the young men to run

11

round the farmstead boundaries holding flaming torches to protect their homes from malevolent spirits[6].

Beltane is named after the God Belenus, a solar God, who was invoked to ensure the good weather and sunlit days of Summer that would result in a rich crop.

At Beltane fertility was at the forefront of people's minds. The God and the Maiden Goddess were married and the marriage consummated. It was expected that in nine months time the new Sun God would be born. (This was also celebrated on March 25th, "Lady Day," which would enable the birth to coincide with Winter Solstice).

During the celebrations the Goddess is celebrated as the May Queen, and the God is the May King, often named Jack in the Green or the Green Man. Maypole dancing represented the unification of the male and female, with the pole symbolising the man, and the ribbons the woman. The ribbons wrap themselves around the man, just as the woman surrounds the man during consummation. Dancing was part of the fertility rites.

It was a time when celebrations were held throughout the villages, and maids and their men folk consummated their relationships without any disapproval. The concept of consummation before marriage was perfectly appropriate, as a wife who could bear children was necessary for the survival of the family line, so the fertility of the woman was tested before the marriage ceremony was held.

At this point the Goddess is still young, but ready to embark on pregnancy and life as a maturing woman. She leaves childhood behind at Beltane and travels the journey of motherhood.

Having initiated your plans in February and March, by May they should be established and taking form. Now is a time to nurture and coax the initial growth into greater maturity. Neglect at this point will not bode well. Rituals held at Beltane invoke fire energy and creativity to your projects, and strength to your healings. Invoke the Goddess of fire and the sun to support and help you.

---

[6]   Freeman (1999)

It is too soon to eat from the present year's harvest, and evenings and days may fluctuate between hot and very cold. Draw on the remnants of last year's produce using nuts and dried fruit, and baking bread and cake. Warm yourself with warm spiced cider or elderberry cordial. Focus on dairy products that would have been in abundance at this time of year in the Iron Age. It is a great time for baking last year's potato crop on the fire, as soon the new potatoes will take their place.

Orange, yellow and red colours support the theme of fire, while green can be used for fertility and balance. Many plants flower at this time and can be gathered fresh from the garden. Hawthorn is in full flower now and traditionally named Mayblossom. Tradition holds that Mayblossom is only picked when in flower. This is the time of greatest and fastest growth, so cutting the Mayblossom for decorating the altar, and invoking its protective qualities is appropriate. The Hawthorn is also one of the hottest burning woods for fires.

LUGHNASADH

Lughnasadh was held as a celebration of the God Lugh who was, "Good at All Things." In Europe he was revered as Lugos, and in Wales he was known as Llew. His festival was important enough to be inscribed on the Calendar of Coligny. The festival became the Christian celebration of the first harvest, and as such was re-named Lammas ("Loaf Mass").

The festival was held on 1st August coinciding with the finish of the grain harvest, when the grain was safely brought in from the fields and stored in barns. After the extremely long hours of physical work the farm owners held celebrations and feasts to reward the helpers who had ensured success.

Abundance is the focus at this time of year. The Mother Goddess has given birth to the harvest and her cornucopia is full. There were many Goddesses of abundance, fertility and the harvest, who were represented carrying cornucopia laden with grain and fruits. Habondia arrived in Britain from Europe, where she was well known and widely worshipped in later centuries. Abundantia was one of the Roman Goddesses of fertility and abundance and migrated to Britain with the Roman invaders. The Three Mothers were well known throughout the Celtic lands, and triplism emphasised their importance.

Think about abundance in your own life. What needs harvesting? What projects and plans have flourished and need to be brought to a close? What is lying around like gleanings for the taking, and will either be taken by someone else, or wasted? Now is the time for thanksgiving. Rituals held simply to give thanks are always joyful occasions. It is also time to face areas of need in your life, and find creative ways to solve problems so that next year's harvest will be fruitful.

Celebrate with grains, bread, cakes, scones, and biscuits, indeed baking of all types. Wine, cider and beer can be drunk, or fruit cordial and herbal teas. Shape homemade bread dough into knots, plaits and circles. Make corn dollies and hang them up to bless the coming year. If you have no straw, use paper craft-straws.

Rituals can be held at noon, the warmest part of the day, when the sun is strong. The flowers are in full bloom and marigolds shine like little suns and compliment the warm spice aromas of orange, bergamot, cinnamon and benzoin. Source "solar" crystals such as sunstone, tiger's eye, red jasper, carnelian and orange and yellow calcite.

Work with the sun at this point in the year. It is a good time to make flower essences and crystal waters. In all things, give thanks.

Festivals in the 21ˢᵗ Century

Celebratory traditions based on the farming calendar have developed and become entrenched in modern society, adopted by Christianity, and fuelled by commercialism. Yule, held at Winter Solstice, is now celebrated as Christmas. Candlemass is celebrated by the Church at Imbolc. Mother's Day, held at the Spring Equinox, is reminiscent of the celebrations for The Great Mother Goddess. Eostre (Ostara) has been reborn as Easter, Samhain is celebrated as Hallowe'en (All Hallows Eve) and in Yorkshire, Yorkshire Day is the 1ˢᵗ of August coinciding with Lughnasadh. This was also celebrated by the church as Lammas. Midsummer is recognised as the longest day (20/21ˢᵗ June) although mostly celebrated in people's gardens with barbeque parties.

THE FOUR CROSS QUARTER FESTIVALS

The festivals of light and dark are much more recent, and have been celebrated as festivals in comparatively modern times as Neo-Wiccan and Neo-Pagan practices flourished in the 20ᵗʰ and 21ˢᵗ centuries. However, these are relevant, and these special times of year were acknowledged by the ancient Brythons, as seen by the orientation of henges, stone circles, tombs and burial chambers that face the rising sun at the Summer and Winter Solstices, or the two Equinoxes.

BALANCING LIGHT AND DARK

The Solstices and Equinoxes were not celebrated as festivals by the ancient Brythons. However, the times of year were acknowledged, especially the Winter Solstice. The Winter was a time of survival and the sun's light became extremely important, the shorter the days became.

We have evidence of the Winter Solstice's importance in the positioning of henges and stone circles, such as Newgrange in Ireland, where the midwinter sunrise lights the interior passage of the grave and is visible for about six days during the Winter Solstice period. The ceremonies focussed on the calling back of the dying sun, and the jubilance of the "resurrection." To these ancients, it meant the continuance of life.

The word "Equinox" means "equal night" and refers to the balance of dark and light. The occurrence of the Equinox is due to the position of the sun above the equator. After this point in time, the light hours increase and dark decreases. Use these times in the year for rituals that promote equality and balance.

SPRING EQUINOX

The Spring Equinox falls around the 20th-21st March and at this point in time the dark hours and light hours are equal, after which the hours of light lengthen until midsummer.

AUTUMN EQUINOX

The Autumn Equinox is held around the 23rd September. At this point in time the light and dark hours are equal, however, soon the dark encroaches, and the length of the hours of darkness increases.

SUMMER SOLSTICE

The Summer Solstice is the lightest point of the year, where the wheel of the year turns towards darkness. In Latin, the word Solstice means "sun stood still," because the sun seems to rise and set in the same place. As we celebrate the longest day, we acknowledge the encroaching darkness and understand that we turn towards the dark months. In rituals acknowledge the power of light and sun and harness this for your purposes. Mythology has it that the Holly King fights the Oak King and wins, bringing on the darker months and declining light.

WINTER SOLSTICE

The Winter Solstice, known as the longest night, is the darkest point of the year. The hours of darkness are greater than at any other time in the year, and in ancient times, it was a matter of trust and faith that the sun would be reborn the next morning. During the Iron Age period, the Celtic people believed their actions could influence the return of the sun, so rituals were held and offerings made to ensure that the sun would rise again.

Yet the Solstice brings hope with the return of the light and the lengthening of the days. Traditionally the Holly King and the Oak King fight again, but this time the Oak King wins, and the wheel continues to turn, bringing the onset of the light months. Turn inward at this time of year and contemplate the mysteries found in the darkness, the unconscious and within oneself. Celebrate the returning sun, and coax it into new birth with fire symbols.

In our Winter Solstice rituals we acknowledge the dying of the light, the sun's descent, and the longest period of darkness. Fertility symbols of the Winter Solstice are holly (masculine), ivy (feminine), evergreen branches, pine cones (masculine) and nuts in shells (feminine).

Rigantona

In my hand, gold and silver entwined,
Sun and moon interwoven,
Turning, circling, encompassing,
Torc of Queens,
Revealed to teach from an earthen grave,
Rigantona rising, age upon age.

A Queen,
Two thousand years ago and more,
Hid her honour,
Placed secrets in the earth,
Dormant, unseen, waiting,
Generation to generation.

Gold-silver filigree,
Link mothers to daughters,
Threads enmeshed,
Turning, circling, encompassing,
This intricate design,
Encircles my heart,
Great Queen,
I honour you.

Ritual for Dedication to the Goddess

Rigantona: The Great Queen

PURPOSE

To dedicate oneself to the Goddess.

This ritual needs preparing in advance. Take time in advance to consider your spiritual beliefs, and how you live your life in accordance with these beliefs. Do they only affect yourself, or do they affect others as well? Why do you believe what you do? Write down a list of beliefs, and what you are able to pledge yourself to. Use the template given in Appendix ii to help.

AIM

To consider what constitutes your belief system. To pledge yourself to living life according to these beliefs. To dedicate oneself to the Goddess for this purpose.

AFFIRMATION

I dedicate myself to the Goddess, Great Queen of the Earth, in beauty and truth.

TIME

Choose the time of year that suits you best. The Summer Solstice on the 21st June, when the hours of light are longest, is a good time to dedicate oneself to the Goddess. The long hours of light can symbolically shine light on your intentions and the solar power available at midsummer, empower your dedication.

However, thinking, questioning, analysing and soul searching works well during the dark months, and the time may be right at the Winter Solstice.

The start of the New Year may be your chosen time, but remember that January 1st is not the only "new year". This is the date of the new year designated by the Gregorian Calendar. In ancient Britain the start of the year was Samhain, 1st November, as the dark half of the year preceded the light half of the year.

Most likely, there will come a point in time when the project feels right for you, and this may be on any day or time of the year.

THE GODDESS

The name Rigantona is a derivation from the Proto-Celtic word Rigani, meaning Great Queen. She was the Great Mother Goddess on whom the Brythons relied for their survival from year to year. As such she was their protectress, midwife, and fertility Goddess who travelled with them through the cycle of the year. She was worshipped as the deity from whom the rivers and springs flowed, the crops grew, the animals produced young, and who was a personification of the Earth itself.

Over many generations, Rigantona's name seems to have developed into the Welsh "Riannon", then respelt "Rhiannon", and her nature absorbed the attributes of the Horse Goddess Epona. By the 21st Century there is a lively debate as to whether Rigantona is the same Goddess as Rhiannon, or Epona, or whether they are separate deities sharing similar iconography. The Goddess Brigantia's name, also meaning "Great Queen" includes the root word "rigan" which translates as "queen".

It may be that Rigantona, The Great Queen, and Epona, the Horse Goddess are separate deities, drawn together through myth and presented as Rhiannon in the Mabinogian (written at a later date of 1066 to 1250 CE).

We will focus on Rigantona as the Goddess of the Land, the Earth, and the people who live from it.

SUBJECT: DEDICATION

Dedicating oneself to a person, a cause, a God or Goddess is a serious business, and cannot be undertaken lightly. For many this ritual may be read, researched and then discarded, because the time is not yet right for dedicating oneself to the Goddess. If this is the case, use the project to examine your beliefs and investigate your understanding of Gods and Goddesses.

Others will substitute the Goddess Rigantona for another of their choice, or have a concept of Divine that is neither male nor female separately. That is fine; adapt this ritual to suit yourself.

For many, this ritual will be used in sincerity after some deep soul searching and analysis of beliefs. When we dedicate ourselves, we need to understand what or who we are dedicating ourselves to. This needs considerable thought and study, research and honesty. After completing research ask yourself if you really believe what you are doing. Do you have idealistic thoughts and theories? Do you believe in archetypes and concepts and give them a name, personifying them?

There is no place for imposing anyone else's ideas here. This needs to be a place of honour and honesty. Use the template to provoke thought and find out what you believe and why. If it is right for you, continue with the ritual.

CORRESPONDENCES

HERBS

Herbs are used to symbolise the elemental energies of air, fire, water and earth, brought together to create life on earth in wholeness. The following herbs are suggestions appropriate for the ritual.

Sage is an herb of Jupiter, the air and the masculine. Sage was understood to be an herb of immortality, longevity, wisdom and protection. It is an herb for making wishes and protecting the body, mind and spirit.

Rosemary is an herb of the Sun, fire and the masculine. Rosemary can be smouldered to rid a place of negative energy, in the same way Sage is used to smudge. Rosemary also protects and helps the memory. It is antiseptic and cleansing, so could be used in the bath of purification before the dedication.

Thyme is an herb corresponding to Venus, water and the feminine. It is used to promote love and healing. Thyme is especially good for nervous disorders, bringing calm and a good night's sleep.

Verbena is an herb corresponding to Venus, earth and the feminine. It is used for purification, protection, to promote healing peaceful sleep, and bring love and money.

Gather it at Midsummer when its powers are strongest.

JEWELLERY

Beautifully crafted jewellery in bronze, silver and gold has been excavated from archaeological digs dating back to the Iron Age. Torcs were worn round the neck and arms, and as they indicated the high rank of a person, the torc was used when carving or casting images of Gods and Goddesses. The Gundstrop Cauldron shows a masculine figure, often named Cernunnos (horned one) wearing one torc round his neck and waving another in his hand.

Jewellery, that was buried in the earth or placed in a bog, river, spring or lake as an offering to the God and Goddess, was often bent or broken in a ritualistic way that suggests that by breaking it in this world's realm it released the item to be used by the God or Goddess to whom it was offered.

EQUIPMENT

The Altar:
    Symbol for the Goddess: large bunch of seasonal flowers and a white candle
    A piece of jewellery or item that symbolises your dedication
    Altar cloth in natural colours, home or handcrafted dyed cloth

The Elements:
    Air and Fire: essential oil diffuser with essential oils of Sage, Rosemary, Thyme and Lemon Verbena
    Water: a bowl of spring water
    Earth: rock salt on a dish

Ritual Items:
    Beliefs and pledges
    Matches

Libation:
    Bread and Wine

The Four Directions: a pot herb
    East : Sage
    South: Rosemary
    West: Thyme
    North: Verbena

THE RITUAL

1. Set up the altar, and place the ritual items next to it.
2. Set the four pots of herbs at each of the four directions.
3. Cast the Circle.
4. Call in the Four Directions:

    Face the East: "I call in the Guardians of the East and the Spirit of Sage, please be witness to this ritual of dedication. Hail and welcome."

    Face the South: "I call in the Guardians of the South and the Spirit of Rosemary, please be witness to this ritual of dedication. Hail and welcome."

    Face the West: "I call in the Guardians of the West and the Spirit of Thyme, please be witness to this ritual of dedication. Hail and welcome."

    Face the North: "I call in the Guardians of the North and the Spirit of Verbena, please be witness to this ritual of dedication. Hail and welcome."

5. Sprinkle a little salt in the water. "I purify this water with the element of earth. I bring earth and water to this ritual. Blessed be."
6. Light the essential oil diffuser. "I bring the element of air and fire to this ritual. Blessed be."
8. Call in the Goddess Rigantona and light her candle:

    "I call in the Goddess Rigantona, the Great Queen, Mother of this Earth, who enables life to continue on Earth. Please be welcome in this circle. Hail and welcome!"

9. State the purpose of the ritual:

    "I dedicate myself to the Great Mother Goddess, the Great Queen, and pledge to live as best I can in beauty and truth according to my beliefs."

10. Raise energy by walking nine times round the circle chanting:

"Rigantona, Great Queen,
Come to this sacred place
Come to me in love and grace
I long to see your face."

Drumming could be used to take you from the normal energies to access the higher, more meditative energies needed for the meditation.

11. Settle down in front of the altar. Make sure you are comfortable and can sit for as long as necessary. Continue to focus on the Goddess.

Take your sheet that you have worked on analysing your beliefs and pledges. Contemplate the reasons you have put down for each.

Is there anything that you want to change? Talk it through with the Goddess.

Decide what you can dedicate yourself to and what you are unsure about. Maybe you cannot dedicate yourself to anything right now. Making promises should not be undertaken lightly. Think about what you are doing at present, and what you can instigate in the near future. Consider where you want to move on to, how will you develop, and what will you do differently. Spend time relating to the Goddess and how she manifests in you and through you.

12. The Dedication (optional)

Turn to face each of the elements in turn starting with air. As you do so, pick up the herb and bring it to the altar.

"I call on the element of air, and the Spirit of Sage, to bear witness to my dedication.

"I call on the element of fire, and the Spirit of Rosemary, to bear witness to my dedication.

"I call on the element of water, and the Spirit of Thyme, to bear witness to my dedication.

"I call on the element of earth, and the Spirit of Verbena, to bear witness to my dedication.

"I dedicate myself to the Great Queen of the Earth, Mother Goddess, from whom all living creatures and plant life has been born and nurtured. I promise to live in beauty and truth, and bring goodness and harmony to the Earth. I pledge to live my life for the highest good, with harm to none, to the best of my ability."

Continue with a more specific and personal dedication. Use your own words.

Dedicate your piece of jewellery as a symbol of your pledge, through the air, fire, water and earth, by moving it over the salt, the water, and the essential oil diffuser for air and fire. This can now be worn when you do further rituals.

13. Give thanks.

14 Spend some time grounding yourself. Now is the time to eat the bread and drink the wine, reserving some for Rigantona. This can be placed outside after closing the circle.

15. Give thanks and say farewell to the Goddess:

"Rigantona, thank you for being part of this ritual. Please help me live each day according to my pledge. Go if you must, stay if you will. Hail and farewell." Blow out the candle.

16. Give thanks and say farewell to the Guardians of the Four Directions and the Herbs of Verbena, Thyme, Rosemary and Sage.

Move to the North: "Guardians of the North and Spirit of Verbena, thank you for being part of this ritual and witnessing my dedication. Go if you must, stay if you will. Hail and farewell."

Move to the West: "Guardians of the West and the Spirit of Thyme, thank you for being part of this ritual and witnessing my dedication. Go if you must, stay if you will. Hail and farewell."

Move to the South: "Guardians of the South and the Spirit of Rosemary, thank you for being part of this ritual witnessing my dedication. Go if you must, stay if you will. Hail and farewell."

Move to the East: "Guardians of the East and the Spirit of Sage, thank you for being part of this ritual and witnessing my dedication. Go if you must, stay if you will. Hail and farewell."

15. Walk round the circle fluffing up the boundary and restoring the space to the physical realm.
16. Place the libation outside on the earth.
17. Plant the herbs in the garden. Tend them carefully, use them for food, infusions, tisanes, and in time, as they grow, bring bundles inside to dry for use in winter.

WHAT TO DO NEXT

Live life with the intention of honouring the Goddess. Be aware of the needs of the Earth from an ecological viewpoint. Uphold your own needs as a woman or man. Explore the nurturing, caring, intuitive, creative aspects of femininity. Also explore the defensive, protecting, guarding, surviving aspects of femininity as well. Wear your jewellery for special spiritual occasions, and let it remind you of this ritual.

MEDITATION

Close your eyes and relax. Breathe deeply in, allowing the air to be drawn right down to your belly. Then let it go very slowly and gently. Repeat this twice more.

Create a protective bubble of white light around yourself. This is a secure place to which you can return at any time. Hold the image in your mind. You are sitting in the very centre, surrounded by white light. This will not let anything harm you. You are protected and safe.

Your safe place shapes itself into a room. It is plain, clean and tidy. Rise from your chair to investigate a wooden door. It is pale oak with a brass handle on it. Walk to the door and push it open. It stays open behind you. Through the door is a stone flagged path bordered by cheerfully coloured flowers. It leads away from the house towards a hazel hedge. There is a gap in the hedge and the path passes straight through. Walk down the path and through the gap in the hazel. Enter the herb garden.

The garden is quite formal in its design with gravel paths between square herb beds. The herbs are all labelled with their name. Walk to the first herb bed you see on your left. Here you find sage. Some sage is silvery green, some dark green and some variegated with green and white leaves.

Touch the sage.

Smell the fragrance.

It is strong but pleasant and clears your throat and nose.

Taste a sage leaf. It feels dry in your mouth. Hold the taste in your mouth.

Focus on the element of air. Consider your relationships with other people. How do you communicate? How do people communicate with you?

Are you finding relationships a blessing, with easy, clear and considerate communication?

Or have people hurt you with their words and actions? Have you upset anyone, intentionally or unintentionally? How can these relationships be improved?

Pick a stem of sage and move to the next herb bed straight ahead of you.

Walk to the second herb bed, and find rosemary. It is spiky and dark green.

Touch the rosemary.

Smell the fragrance.

It is peppery, warming and stimulating. It clears your mind and helps you concentrate.

Taste a rosemary leaf. It is crisp, chewy and strong flavoured. Hold the taste in your mouth.

Focus on the element of fire. Consider your creativity. What do you create? What would you like to create? Are you happy and content with the life you have created for yourself or do you want to make changes? What can you do enable your creativity to flourish?

Pick a stem of rosemary and move to the next herb bed. Turn to the right and walk straight ahead.

At the third herb bed you find thyme.

Touch the thyme.

Smell the fragrance.

It is clean and fresh smelling.

Taste a thyme leaf. It has a delicate texture and a fragrant flavour. Hold the taste in your mouth.

Focus on the element of water. Consider your emotions. Are you calm and balanced? Or do your emotions swing from ecstatic highs to depressive lows? Who do you love, and who loves you? Family, friends, lovers. Are you confident and secure or frightened easily and anxious? Can your emotional balance be improved? Do you need help and where will you seek help?

Pick a stem of thyme and move clockwise to the fourth and last herb bed. Walk straight ahead.

At the fourth herb bed you find verbena.

Touch the verbena.

Smell the fragrance.

It is earthy yet light and fragrant.

Taste the verbena. It is savoury and nourishing. Hold the taste in your mouth.

You focus on the element of earth. Consider your physical well being. Are you healthy and well? Do you exercise, eat well and sleep soundly? Or do you struggle to maintain your health? Do you eat foods that nourish you? Do you seek out herbs, spices and vegetables that keep your body balanced? Are there changes you need to make to your lifestyle to help your body cope with 21st century living?

Pick a sprig of verbena.

Hold your bunch of herbs: sage, rosemary, thyme and verbena.

Breathe sage in, and breathe it out.

Breathe rosemary in, and breathe it out.

Breathe thyme in, and breathe it out.

Breathe verbena in, and breathe it out.

Place the sprigs in a bunch and take them back to the garden path.

Walk through the gap in the hazel hedge. Holding your bundle of herbs, you feel strengthened and empowered by them. Walk between the flower borders, back to the house door, where it stands open welcoming you.

Enter the room, and sit on your chair. Breathe in the herbal fragrance of your bundle of herbs deeply, and release.

Breathe in peace, and release

Breathe in joy, and release

Breathe in love, and release

When you are ready, open your eyes.

You are back. Welcome home.

Elen

You have walked through centuries
Rough tracks and mountain paths
On wooden boardwalks across wetlands
Over moorland hills, along dark forest paths.
By mountain streams climbing to the marsh
Land that gives birth to the gurgling infant spring.

If I could hold onto the edge of your cloak
You would lead me through countless seasons,
Year upon year they change
The ground that lies under your feet.

From under the hem of your skirt emerge
Snowdrops and aconites,
Grasses and ferns,
Sapling trees bend in the wind.

All around you beech and hazel shed their nuts.
You plant the acorn; I watch it grow.

Walk with me as I journey,
Breathing hard, climb rugged hills,
Guide me through dangerous water,
Reveal the place of rest,
You have walked this way before,
My journey has begun.

Ritual for Blessing New Resolutions

Elen of the Ways:
she of the roads and trackways

Goddess of the Welsh borders

PURPOSE

To bless the journey through the coming year, form intentions and resolutions, and make plans for the year to come.

AIM

Pine cones are used to carry written intentions, resolutions and plans into the fire to be offered up for the blessing of Elen. The pine cones symbolise the old year, and the emptiness as the year comes to a closure, and the written tickets represent the future that is energised by the element of fire.

AFFIRMATION

My intentions, resolutions and plans are coming to fruition.

TIME

New Year's Eve, or New Year's Day, January.

THE GODDESS

Elen is the Goddess of journeys, and the roads, paths and trackways that make journeys possible. In Britain we still find Ellie stones, and Elen's causeway. Elen is the Goddess who keeps the cycles of nature in balance, and ensures continued fertility.

Elen is found in the Mabinogian, in the tale of Breuddwyd Mascen as "Elen of Hosts." During a hunt, in the heat of the day, at noon, Mascen dozes and dreams of Elen, falling hopelessly in love with the beautiful woman that he sees sitting on her red-gold throne. Mascen awakes, and longing for the woman in his dream, sends search parties out to seek her. They eventually find her, seated on her red-gold throne, but she says that if Mascen wants her so much, he must come himself. He travels on a long journey to find her, and after many adventures, finds her and she marries him. For her wedding gift she asks for the authority to build roads between three cities, which enables the defence of those cities and the surrounding district. She becomes known as Elen Lwydogg, "Elen of Hosts". These roads remain today, named "Sarn Helen".

Helen is the Greek word for "torch". The torches of the Greek processions were made from the pine tree. The tear droplets of resin that the pine and the silver birch trees release, feeds the fly agaric fungus that was ingested by the shamanic sages to support and aid their astral journeys. The deer that formed the ancient trackways in the Stone Age and Bronze Age times ate the fly agaric, and the residue is traceable in their droppings. For this reason the ancient deer tracks can be traced in the modern day.

There are many other references to Elen, including Elen, the daughter of King Cole (Coel), who was a tribal chief of Colchester. She also metamorphosed into St Helena, the mother of Constantine the Great, and the wife of Emperor Constantias Chlorus. However, this link with Elen of the Ways is tenuous. St Helena's day is held by the church on 22nd May.

Whether you are making journeys in the physical realm, from place to place, using modern transport, or ancient tracks, or whether you are journeying on your life path, making decisions, fulfilling plans and completing resolutions, Elen of the Ways, is the Goddess to turn to for help.

SUBJECT: JOURNEYS

Life is a journey, and unless we move forward, we can get stuck in a rut, or even start moving backwards. When was the last time you challenged yourself with something new? Do you know where your life is heading, or is your life stagnant? Do you want to progress, develop and change? Use this ritual to investigate where your life journey is heading and what changes are needed to accommodate the next step forward.

CORRESPONDENCES

FIR CONES

Conifers are evergreen trees found throughout Europe. They are long lived trees that tend to grow on higher ground, and are protected for the most part by thick bark. Their branches form spirals round the trunk, and the pattern of branch spirals, needles and cone scales follows the Fibonacci number ratios. Conifers produce male and female cones. The male cones are small and fall to the ground after shedding pollen. The female cones are larger and take up to three years to mature after pollination. The seeds are dispersed by the winds.

TRACKWAYS

During the Bronze Age trackways were built from timber across bog land and wet areas. One such example is the track way running between Ponden Hills and Meare Island that has been excavated by the Somerset Levels Project. Base oak sleepers were held in place by pairs of long oak stakes and the walkway itself was built from wide oak planks. Excavation has shown that during the Bronze Age the land was arable pasture and woodland. The area was initially wet but may have been flooded, and the raised track built in response to enable access to the farm land.

WASSAIL

The Wassail Cup was a bowl of spiced ale that was passed from person to person during the New Year merrymaking, with the salutation, "Wass hael!" "Wass hael" is the ancient Saxon for, "To your health!" The local poor took a decorated bowl from house to house to collect money and join their rich neighbours for a drink. Many songs arose from the Wassail tradition including the famous Gloucester Wassail and the Gower Wassail.

EQUIPMENT

The Altar:
   Symbol for the Goddess: a pile of fir cones and a green candle
   Altar cloth in colours of green, brown, and red

The Elements:
   Air: an essential oil diffuser and essential oil of pine
   Fire and Water: a bowl of spring water and some floating candles
   Earth: rock salt on a dish

Ritual Items:
    Pine cones
    Paper tickets
    Pen
    Hearth fire, or a fire pit outside
    Charcoal, matches, firelighters

Libation:
    Fruit cake and mulled red wine
    Pan
    Wassail mug

The Four Directions:
    East: yellow candle
    South: red candle
    West: blue candle
    North: green candle

THE RITUAL

1. Set up the altar, and place the ritual items next to it.
2. Set the four candles at each of the four directions.
3. Cast the Circle.
4. Call in the Four Directions:

    Face the East: "As I travel to the East, I call in the Guardians of the East. Hail and welcome."

    Light the yellow candle.

    Face the South: "As I travel to the South, I call in the Guardians of the South. Hail and welcome."

    Light the red candle.

    Face the West: "As I travel to the West, I call in the Guardians of the West. Hail and welcome."

    Light the blue candle.

Face the North: "As I travel to the North, I call in the Guardians of the North. Hail and welcome."

Light the green candle.

5. Sprinkle a little salt in the water and light the floating candles. "I purify this water with the element of earth. I bring earth and water to this ritual. Blessed be."

6. Light the incense. "I bring the element of air to this ritual. Blessed be."

7. Stand in front of the fire and light it. "I bring the element of fire to this ritual. Blessed be."

8. Call in the Goddess Elen of the Trackways and light the green candle.

    "I call in the Goddess, Elen of the Trackways, the Lady who built roads and tracks across the wilderness, and enabled people to make journeys. Please be welcome in this circle. I ask your loving blessing on this ritual. May it be for the highest good of all. Hail and welcome!"

9. State the purpose of the ritual. "This ritual is to bring blessing to the journey through the next year and to form intentions and resolutions, and make plans for the year to come."

10. State the affirmation. "My plans, intentions and resolutions are coming to fruition."

11. Raise energy by walking nine times round the circle chanting:

"Elen of the roads and trackways,
Bring your blessing to this year's journey,
As I walk along my path,
Guard, protect and direct me."

Feel the energy build up, the expectation of a good result strengthen, and the power of the Goddess become manifest.

12. Settle in front of the hearth or fire pit.

    Write down a resolution, a plan or an intention on a piece of paper, fold it and place within a pine cone. Hold it. Understand that the old year is now empty, yet it holds the future, just as the pine cone that is empty of seeds, now holds your written resolution, plan or intention. Throw it on the fire and let it burn.

One by one, do the same with all your intentions, resolutions, and plans.

Keep the fire stoked. When you have finished give thanks. Write a thank you note and place it in a pine cone and put on the fire. You may want to write, "So mote it be," on your last paper for your last cone. Burn it as an offering to Elen.

13. Now it is time to eat the fruit cake and drink the Wassail cup.

     Place your mulled wine mix on the fire. Warm it through. Pour it into a Wassail Cup (mug, chalice, glass). Bless the drink and bless the cake. Sprinkle a little cake on the soil, and moisten the ground with a little mulled wine as a libation.

     Eat and drink and enjoy the sensation of completing the ritual. If you are with friends, pass round the "Wassail Cup" wishing each other a happy new year.

14. Give thanks and say farewell to the Goddess:

     "Lady Elen, Goddess of journeys, roads and trackways, I thank you for being part of this ritual and bestowing your blessing on my intentions, resolutions and plans. Go if you must, stay if you will. Hail and farewell." Put out the green candle and extinguish the floating candles.

15. Give thanks and say farewell to the Spirits of the Four Directions.

     Move to the North: "Spirit of the North and the Earth, thank you for being part of this ritual and blessing my new project. Go if you must, stay if you will. Hail and farewell." Blow out the green candle.

     Move to the West: "Spirit of the West and Water, thank you for being part of this ritual and blessing my new project. Go if you must, stay if you will. Hail and farewell." Blow out the blue candle.

Move to the South: "Spirit of the South and Fire, thank you for being part of this ritual and blessing my new project. Go if you must, stay if you will. Hail and farewell." Blow out the red candle.

Move to the East: "Spirit of the East and Air, thank you for being part of this ritual and blessing my new project. Go if you must, stay if you will. Hail and farewell." Blow out the yellow candle.

16. Walk round the circle fluffing up the boundary and restoring the space to the physical realm.

17. Place the libation outside.

18. Stay with the fire until it has burnt out or put the fire out safely. When cold, place the ashes on the soil to nourish the ground.

WHAT TO DO NEXT

Plans do not fulfil themselves without the author's intervention. Having affirmed the plans, intentions and resolutions, and received the blessing for them, then it is time to take the action necessary to make them happen. Blessing is received in many ways: coincidental meetings, enthusiastic encouragement, support and help, and the smooth running as plans are executed. Hitches are overcome and the determination to bring the plan to closure is found within oneself.

Make a timeline for the weeks and months ahead, and place on it your intentions to start projects or resolutions. Further down the timeline, mark the expected time for finishing the project and achieving the resolutions.

If you are handy with a spreadsheet, list the weeks or months across the top, one in each column, and the plan, project, resolution down the left hand side. A note is then placed where the "Plan Row" intersects with the "Date Column". Lines can be drawn to link the start, the finish and any other actions that impinge on the first. Being computerised intended events can be moved, leading to realistic flexibility.

MEDITATION

Close your eyes and relax. Breathe deeply in, allowing the air to be drawn right down to your belly. Then let it go very slowly and gently. Repeat this twice more.

Create a protective bubble of white light around yourself. This is a secure place to which you can return at any time. Hold the image in your mind. You are sitting in the very centre, surrounded by white light. This will not let anything harm you. You are protected and safe.

Put on walking boots, sturdy but soft. Tie the laces securely and stand up. You are dressed warmly but comfortably, suitable for a winter's walk. Pick up a shoulder bag and place five quartz crystals into it.

Leave your safe place through a wooden door and find yourself in a forest of conifers. Tall pine trees spread in all directions. You notice pines, larch, fir, slender trunks reaching skywards, and through the canopy of needles you see the pale blue sky and the winter sun.

Follow the path ahead, walking softly on a carpet of fallen needles, releasing the invigorating perfume of pine.

You see fallen pine cones and pick one up. Look at the spiral of the cone scales. The seeds have fallen or been collected by squirrels. Follow the pattern with your finger from the base of the cone, spiralling into the centre at the peak of the cone.

Consider your life's journey. Do you envisage it as a straight path, or does it spiral round and around, revisiting issues and concepts, and allowing you to experience them with growing knowledge, understanding and wisdom.

Put the pine cone in your bag, and place a quartz crystal at the base of a tree. Give the tree and the earth a blessing.

Walk down the path until you come to a clearing in the forest. Here you find a rocky granite plateau with grasses and ferns growing between the rocks. Pick up a piece of granite from between some rocks. Feel the rough surface with your fingers and see how the quartz inclusions sparkle in the winter sun. Feel the weight of the rock and tune into the rock's spirit.

Contemplate the ancient rock and the rocks from which it has parted. The rock has been here since the beginning of time, and now you can touch it, feel it and connect with it. The rock imparts a sense of the eternal, as well as the passage of time.

Put the rock in your bag, and place a quartz crystal between the rocks on the plateau. Give the rocks and the earth a blessing.

Follow the path between the rocks until it becomes steeper underfoot. Step carefully. You climb uphill. Smaller deciduous trees edge the path: hawthorn and rowan. Look carefully at a rowan tree and see a clump of red wrinkled berries hanging from a branch. Pick the berries and look at their crimson wrinkled skins. Think about the aging process and the way in which you, yourself will age. It is part of the journey of life and part of the wheel of the year: birth, youth, maturity, aging, and death. This is followed in the annual cycle by rebirth and growth. The wheel turns again. Squash one of the berries and look at the seeds within, full of potential life.

Put the rowan berries in your bag, and place a quartz crystal in the tree where the branch meets the trunk. Give the rowan and the earth a blessing.

Climb up beside a mountain stream until you reach a wooden plank bridge spanning the stream. Lean against the handrails and look down into the turbulent waters below. The water tumbles, turns, rolls and froths around boulders, rocks and stones. It gives life to the plants, ferns and trees, whose roots delve deep into the damp banks of the stream.

Look at an overhanging branch with a solitary golden leaf hanging from it. You pick the leaf and look at its texture, noticing the veins that run from the central line to the outer edges. You think of the energy that flows through you bringing vitality and health to your body. Feel the energy flowing, up from the earth, through your feet, up your body and round your head. It flows down your arms and into your hands.

Put the leaf into your bag, and throw a quartz crystal into the mountain stream. Give the water and the earth a blessing.

Cross the bridge and make your way downstream. Soon the path broadens into a well defined gravel track. The stream is widening into a river, becoming broader, deeper and smoother.

Walk by the edge of the river, by a ploughed field of rich earth waiting for the spring sowing. Pick up some soil and rub it between your fingers. Sense its potential for nurturing life.

Think about the fertility of the land and the nurturing energy the earth gives us. No wonder we call her Mother Earth.

You sprinkle the soil in a pocket of your bag, and place a quartz crystal into the earth. Give the earth a blessing.

Follow the path away from the field into the forest again. Through the pines and firs you see a log cabin nestling between two guardian pines. The door is half open and looks inviting. Enter the log cabin and find yourself back in your safe place.

Sit down in your safe place. Think about your journey, through the pine trees, over the rocks, uphill by the mountain stream, over the wooden bridge and down through the ploughed field. Give thanks for the way the earth sustains us and helps us on our own journey of birth, growth, transformation and rebirth.

Take the gifts of the journey, the pine cone, the rock, the rowan berries, the golden leaf and the rich soil deep into your soul.

Breathe in peace, and release

Breathe in joy, and release

Breathe in love, and release

When you are ready, open your eyes.

You are back. Welcome home.

Brigantia

The dark days are over,
Warmth and light approach,
Growth and fruition contained,
In the smallest seed.

The seed lies in my heart,
I water it with tears,
Feed it with compassion,
Nurture it with love.
Protected, my seedling grows strong
and straight.

Envisage the harvest,
Fruit repays labour,
Creation brings forth life,
We reside in the kernel,
Known by our fruit.

Ritual to Bring Blessing to Friends and Family

Brigantia: she who brings Spring renewal

Goddess of Northern England

PURPOSE

To bless me, my family and friends with positive energy for our highest good.

AIM

To make a cairn of tumblestones, each one energised with a blessing for you, a family member or a friend. To release the blessing for the highest good.

AFFIRMATION

My family, friends and I, benefit from the surging energy of Spring, and the blessing it brings.

TIME

Imbolc, 2nd February.

THE GODDESS

Brigantia is the Goddess of the Brigantes, a tribe known simply as the "Great Tribe," just as Brigantia is the "Great Queen". She is synonymous with Bride, Brigit, Bridget—many names for the same fire Goddess of the emerging spring. She is the Goddess of the land, the Spring time, and the energy of new growth. She is the Goddess of the bulbs that push through frost and snow and flower regardless. She is the Goddess of the new born lambs and the very first ewe's milk of the year. These are the signs that the darkest days of the year are over and the light is beginning to dominate.

The Brigantes tribe were a large group comprising many different, smaller tribes, situated over the northern Pennines and into Cumbria. Brigantia was invoked as *Deae Nymphae Brigantiae* in Irthington, Cumbria and Brampton in Cumberland. Inscriptions have been found at South Shields, in County Durham, and in Adel and Castleford in North Yorkshire.

In the northern region of Yorkshire, the mountain Ingleborough forms part of the Three Peaks range. The other mountains in the range are Whernside and Pennyghent, and the challenge is to climb all three in a day. On the summit of Ingleborough are found what may be the foundations of Bronze or Iron Age huts within a fortification wall. "Borough" developed from the Old English word "burh" meaning "fort on the hill." It suggests Ingleborough was named after an ancient fortress built on the visual advantage point on high ground, to protect the surrounding fertile area.

The hill fort may have been known as "The King's Fort" to the Romans. Many stones have been moved, but the defensive wall can still be found. A large cairn has been built on top of Ingleborough, and from that stone-built construction of modern times, we take our inspiration for the ritual.

Nearby, on the outskirts of Settle is the lovely Scalebar Foss. This beautiful waterfall flows down a small rocky ravine, known as a "linn", changing direction with every drop, and enhanced by the cloak of green mosses which cover the limestone rocks. This seems to personify the wildness, the elemental freedom of Brigantia, yet is highly accessible to visitors from the road. A rich botanical environment of moss and ferns thrives in this damp area. From Ingleton one can take the "Waterfall Walk" and indulge in spectacular scenery with rare plants and ancient oak woodland.

Here we can experience the essence of ancient Brigantia, wildness, an elemental force, the regeneration of life, and the spark of life that keeps us invigorated.

SUBJECT: BLESSING

When we send a blessing to someone, we are sending positive energy for that person's highest good. We do not always know what is best for a person and so often as not, we send general good wishes to the person in the hope that they will benefit. In this ritual we only work for a person's highest good, sending them positive energy that will do them good.

CORRESPONDENCES

CAIRNS

Cairns are way markers, built to mark the pathways over the mountains, hills and high ground at times of the year when the path is lost to view under snow. Climbers make cairns by adding a stone to a summit pile when they have climbed to the top of a hill or mountain. It is a way of celebrating and acknowledging the achievement. Cairns can be seen from a long distance away and mark some of the highest areas of land.

SNOWDROPS

Snowdrops are Britain's first flower of the Spring. They survive January snow and push up through the frozen soil to herald the way into the warmer months.

EQUIPMENT

The Altar:
> A symbol of the Goddess: a white candle
> Altar cloths in pale green and white
> A vase of snowdrops
> A pot of bulbs, already growing

The Elements:
> Air: an essential oil diffuser and essential oils of lemon and thyme
> Fire: white candle
> Water: white dish of water
> Earth: white plate of rock salt

Ritual Items:
> A pile of tumblestones
> A white plate

Libation:
> White bread, oat cakes, sheep's cheese and a glass of milk

The Four Directions:

    East: yellow candle and a yellow crystal

    South: red candle and red crystal

    West: blue candle and blue crystal

    North: green candle and green crystal

THE RITUAL

1. Set up the altar, and place the ritual items next to it.
2. Set the four candles and crystals at each of the four directions.
3. Cast the Circle.
4. Call in the Four Directions:

   Face the East: "I call in the Spirit of Spring and new growth. Hail and welcome." Light the yellow candle.

   Face the South: "I call in the Spirit of Summer and the growing crops, vegetables, fruit and flowers. Hail and welcome." Light the red candle.

   Face the West: "I call in the Spirit of Autumn and the harvests of grain and fruit. Hail and welcome." Light the blue candle.

   Face the North: "I call in the Spirit of Winter when the land is dormant, but Snowdrops push through the soil to bloom. Hail and welcome." Light the green candle.

5. Sprinkle a little salt in the water. "I purify this water with the element of earth. I bring earth and water to this ritual. Blessed be."
6. Light the incense. "I bring the element of air to this ritual. Blessed be."
7. Light the white candle. "I bring the element of fire to this ritual. Blessed be."
8. Call in the Goddess Brigantia and light her white candle.

   "I call in the Goddess Brigantia, she who brings renewal, and blessings, please be welcome in this circle. I ask your loving blessing on this ritual. May it be for the highest good of all. Hail and welcome!"

9. State the purpose of the ritual:
   "This ritual is to bless me, my family and friends with positive energy for their highest good."

10. Raise energy by walking nine times round the circle chanting:

> *"Brigantia of the northern land,*
> *Through hills and dales nine times around,*
> *Bless me, my friends and family,*
> *I invoke thee, three times three."*

Feel the energy build up, the expectation of a good result strengthen, and the power of the Goddess become manifest.

11. Settle in front of the altar and pick up one tumblestone at a time. Visualise your family member or friend. Bless them and intend the blessing to enter and be invigorated by the crystal. Put it on the white plate and start to build your cairn.

    As you pick up crystals, and invoke positive energy and blessings for your family and friends, adding them to the pile on the white plate, you gradually build a cairn of stones. Finish the cairn with a tumblestone blessed for you.

    Dedicate the finished cairn to Brigantia and move it through the elements of air, fire, water and earth. State the affirmation: "My family, friends and I benefit from the surging energy of Spring, and the blessing it brings."

12. Now is the time to eat the bread and cheese, and drink the milk, reserving some for Brigantia. This can be laid outside after closing the circle.

13. Give thanks and say farewell to the Goddess:
    "Brigantia, I thank you for being part of this ritual and bestowing your blessing on my family and friends. Go if you must, stay if you will. Hail and farewell." Put out the white candles.

14. Give thanks and say farewell to the Spirits of the Four Directions.

    Move to the North: "Spirit of Winter when the land is dormant, but Snowdrops push through the soil to bloom, go if you must, stay if you will. Hail and farewell." Blow out the green candle.

    Move to the West: "Spirit of Autumn and the harvests of grain and fruit, go if you must, stay if you will. Hail and farewell." Blow out the blue candle.

    Move to the South: "Spirit of Summer and the growing crops, vegetables, fruit and flowers, go if you must, stay if you will. Hail and farewell." Blow out the red candle.

    Move to the East: "Spirit of Spring and new growth, go if you must, stay if you will. Hail and farewell." Blow out the yellow candle.

15. Walk round the circle fluffing up the boundary and restoring the space to the physical realm.

16. Place the libation outside.

17. Leave the cairn in a safe place and let the crystals send the energy out and work on behalf of your family and friends. You may wish to leave it outside.

WHAT TO DO NEXT

Become a blessing to your family and friends. Often we answer our own prayers ourselves. As we generate kindness, generosity and love, so this is amplified and ripples outwards into the world. We receive back as much as we give.

MEDITATION

Close your eyes and relax. Breathe deeply in, allowing the air to be drawn right down to your belly. Then let it go very slowly and gently. Repeat this twice more.

Create a protective bubble of white light around yourself. This is a secure place to which you can return at any time. Hold the image in your mind. You are sitting in the very centre, surrounded by white light. This will not let anything harm you. You are protected and safe.

Your safe place shapes itself into a garden. It is early Spring and you can see crocus, daffodils and grape hyacinth blooming under trees that will fruit in the Summer. At the end of the garden there is a small wooden gate. Walk through the gate and see a broad path leading towards a mountain. At first it is edged with hawthorn bushes, hazel and ash trees. Then the path narrows and leads you through grassy pasture, up the shoulder of the mountain into higher moorland.

Follow the path, climbing upwards, between trees, over the pasture and up to the granite boulders in the moorland. Climb, taking in deep breathes of clean, fresh air and feel invigorated.

You reach a large plateau. Stop here for a rest and look out over the valleys and hills, as far as the sea.

Become aware of houses, cities, gardens

See your family

. . . and your friends

Who are your real friends?

Name them

Climbing upwards from the plateau the path is steep and rocky. It is hard work, but every time you want to stop and turn back, you find a hand hold, or a foot hold, or a flat rock to rest on. Take your time. Rest a little and catch your breath.

Now climb with determination, holding the names of your family and friends in your heart. You reach the top and see a great cairn surrounded by stones. Find a flat rock by the cairn and rest. Look around at the stones on the ground. Take one stone for each family member and each friend and place it on the cairn. As you do so name your family member or friend and send them love, healing, and blessings. Place a final stone on the cairn for yourself.

As you look at the cairn, and the shapes of the stones as they fit together, you become aware of the body and face of a woman emerging from the rocks. She is rugged, as old as the earth. Is she rock? Or plants? Lichens and moss? Is she soil, earth, animal or bird? Insect or . . . . is she found in the wind? It is Brigantia, Goddess of the land.

For a moment she comes to you, meets with you, face to face, forehead to forehead, she reaches into you, becomes you, and you are part of her. Feel her ancient energy and know that she will send your family and friends that which they need most.

Then she fades from you and you feel the soft wind on your face, the ground under your feet. Climb down the mountain slowly but steadily.

Walk down from the moorland, over the pasture land and between the hawthorn and hazel hedges. Dry stone walls replace the hedges, and then you see a wooden five bar gate across the lane. The gate swings open easily, and as you go through the gate, find yourself in your safe place.

Sit in your safe place.

Breathe in peace, and release

Breathe in joy, and release

Breathe in love, and release

You are ready to open your eyes.

You are back. Welcome home.

Arnemetia

Sacred grove of silver birches,
Ladies reaching to the sky,
Silver sun shines bright on snowfall,
Snow on heather, snow on rock.

Winter light is waning quickly,
Drawing darkness, shadows form,
Sunlight, through the branches dropping,
Descends into sleep.

Nine rock maidens form a circle,
Dance together beneath the moon,
The King alone, stands forlornly,
Shadows from a distant time.

Silver moon and nine stones gleaming,
One woman lays down her ring,
Lays it on the north stone, standing,
Sacrificial offering.

The lone woman lays down her flowers,
Kneels and weeps, then laughs and smiles,
Fraught with loves, and disappointments,
Lays down her heart tonight.

Silver light on nine stones scatters,
Catches the flowers and the ring,
Illuminates the grove with splendour,
Reflecting off the trees.

Goddess in the grove is dreaming,
Silver shining from the ring,
Woman walks the nine stones, nine times,
Wakes the Goddess from her sleep.

Goddess of the birch grove watching,
Woman bows her head to leave,
Goddess makes the unearthly promise,
"Rest in sacred peace."

Woman walking quickly homewards,
Ring and flowers are left in place,
Left to please the nine stones' Goddess,
Of this sacred place.

Ritual for Dedicating a New Project

Arnemetia: she who dwells by the Sacred Grove

Goddess of Buxton, Derbyshire

PURPOSE

To bring vibrant new energy to action a new project.

AIM

To create a symbolic stone circle using crystal points, and within the stone circle, to grow seeds, watered by sun and moon energised water. This symbolises the initiation and new growth of the project energised by the stones and blessed by the Goddess.

A small amount of preparation is needed in advance. Make a balancing, harmonizing water by mixing equal parts of Sun and Moon water. (See Appendix iii).

AFFIRMATION

My new project is conceived, rooted, and grows fruitfully.

TIME

The Spring Equinox, March

THE GODDESS

Arnemetia was the local Goddess of the town now known as Buxton in Derbyshire. It is thought that the local tribe, the Corieltauvi worshipped her long before the Romans invaded the area. During the Roman invasion and settlement, the town was known as Aquae Arnemetia and was large enough and important enough for three baths and a shrine to be built. The only other town in Britain important enough to be given the designation "Aquae" was Aquae Sulis, the present-day Bath. The local Celts did not worship inside buildings; that was a custom for the Romans. Instead they chose the woods and the trees for their sacred temples. A "nemeton" was a sacred grove, and it was amongst the trees of the sacred grove that the Druids invoked their Gods and Goddesses and held rituals for the local tribal people. The name Arnemetia means, "She who dwells in front of the Sacred Grove."

SUBJECT: PROJECTS

Projects have a start and a finish. They are creative, but need thorough planning and organisation to bring them from the initial concept through to the tangible stage where the project can be released as a finished product or performance. Projects often develop in stages, and need focus and discipline to ensure that the creative inspiriation materialises in concrete form. Whether your project is a work of art, a skill to learn, a production to create and perform, or an improvement to society, Arnemetia can help you to fulfil your project.

CORRESPONDENCES

STONE CIRCLES

Exploring the surrounding area in modern times, one finds Mesolithic and Bronze Age ancient sites, such as the Nine Ladies of Stanton Moor, a circle of nine small stones set among the silver birch woods on the top of the moor. The henge and stone circle at Arbor Low are easily accessible, and given the bunch of flowers, decorated Ostara (Easter) eggs, and symbols on the henge sides, it can be presumed that the henge is still used by 21st century pagans. Stoke Flatt is a small stone circle on Froggatt Edge, which has unusual double stone markers in the perimeter. Nine Stones Close (Grey Ladies) can be found without difficulty, although only four of the nine original stones remain. Towering above Nine Stones Close is the site of an Iron Age rock fortress and the Hermitage. There are many more examples in the area, though some are less easily found and accessed. These are the Bronze Age sacred sites of people who worshipped the Goddess, although it is not known if Arnemetia was named and celebrated at this point in time.

SACRED SPRINGS

In Buxton, today, warm spring water emerges at 28° Celsius from St Anne's Well. St Anne is thought to be the Christianised assimilation and transmutation of the Goddess Arnemetia[7] although there is no direct proof. The healing spring of St Anne was established earlier than the foundation of the cult of St Anne, which was documented in the fourteenth century. The water can be drunk straight from source at the present day spring, though this was moved from its original position

---

[7]   Morrell *(1994)*

when Buxton was developed as a spa town. It contains minerals because the water has filtered through the limestone rock formations of the White Peak district, and it is said that these minerals help arthritis and rheumatic conditions, along with many other everyday ills. This is the local belief, straight from the mouth of a Buxton resident who collects water every day and drinks it for his health. In the Iron Age era water was considered magical and sacred. It was conceived of as a healing element, and in Buxton the water from the springs was used for healing disease. The Iron Age people were comparatively keen on cleanliness, and also used water for washing. Water, wells and natural springs are still celebrated in Derbyshire with the local Well Dressing Festivals held during the Spring and Summer months of the year.

NUMBER NINE

Nine is the number of completion, the number reached before returning to the beginning of the cycle of numbers from 1 to 9. In Numerology life is measured in phases of 9, 18. 27, 36, 45, 54, 63, 72, 81, 90, 99, 108 and for those who reach this grand number of years, 117. It is the number that resonates with a concern for the betterment of the world. It is an idealistic number, denoting selflessness, generosity, nobleness and a compassionate attitude. People who have the number 9 in their Numerology chart tend to have a universal love of life, a benevolent attitude and a sense of tolerance and forgiveness. Creativity is predominant, along with romance and passion.

THE SPRING EQUINOX

The official date for the Spring Equinox is March 21st, and is the time when the Sun enters Aries and is positioned above the Equator. Aries is ruled by Mars, the God and planet of fire and the symbol of Aries is the Ram. It is the start of Spring in Britain, when light and dark are held in perfect balance. Harmony and equilibrium are the order of the day and night, and the Goddess is in her Virgin aspect, unmarried, yet mature enough to join sexually with the Young God and conceive a child. The new God will be born on 21st December, at the Winter Solstice, thus symbolising the start of the increase of light for the next year.

Traditionally, the conception is recognised on 25th March, Lady Day, and celebrated separately. Other auspicious dates that are recognised are Ostara (Germanic) and Eostre (Saxon) held on the first full moon after the Equinox, and Easter (Christian) held on the first Sunday, after the full moon, after the Equinox. Druids celebrate "Alban Eiler", their name for the Spring Equinox. Alba means white, and Eil means "Light". The high point in the Druid's Wheel of the Year stands in the East, where the Sun rises. Alban Eiler is the start of the Druid New Year, and it honours The Lady, who contains the Lord of Light and all of Life. It is he who makes the stand against the dark. Together the Lord of Light and The Lady create a mystical union, and equally partnered, they bring new life.

EQUIPMENT

The Altar:

Symbol for the Goddess: a large bunch of budding daffodils

Altar cloths in colours of yellow, orange, green and white

Flower buds and fresh herbs

Yellow crystals

The Elements:

Air: essential oil diffuser and essential oils

Fire: yellow candle

Water: Sun and Moon water mixed in equal parts in a jug

Earth: rock salt on a dish

Ritual Items:

Nine quartz crystal points

Circular pot

Seed compost

Packet of seeds

Matches

The Four Directions:

As Arnemetia is known as the "Lady who dwells against the sacred grove", the four directions are symbolised by tree energy. Collect four types of tree branches and twigs. Make a bundle of twigs for each of the directions and bind together with ribbon. The following are recommended if available:

East: Hazel

Hazel is a feminine tree, corresponding to the element of air, and the fresh wind that blows across the Peak District from the Pennines. It is found in many areas of the White Peak District where the underlying rock is limestone, and amongst open woodland and on the edges of woods. The forked branches of Hazel were used for divination, to find water and also to distinguish between criminals and innocent people. Hazels find their place in the Mabinogian where nine Hazels grow by the Well of Segais, and drop their hazel nuts into the water. The salmon that swims in the water has nine spots, one for each of the filberts (nuts) of wisdom it has swallowed. Concentrated wisdom is symbolised in the encased sweetness of the filberts. Hazels are known bringers of luck and a necklace of hazelnuts used to be hung in houses to bring good fortune. Hazel relates to the ninth moon of the Roman calendar year, between August 5th and September 1st, and is linked to the planet Mercury.

South: Hawthorn

Hawthorn is a masculine tree, and corresponds to the element of fire. Hawthorn wood fires are the hottest fire known. The tree offers protection, and ancient lore advises never to cut it and bring it indoors or it will bring bad luck. Hawthorn clears away old stagnant energy helping bring clear, fresh insight. In many areas of Britain it is commonly used to denote field boundaries, and provides a whitewash of Mayblossom in late April and early May. However, the White Peak countryside is bounded by dry stone walling given the limestone rocks and stones available to the farmers. The word "Huath" means "hard" or "sharp" relating to the wood and the thorns. Hawthorn relates to the sixth moon of the Roman calendar year, between May 13th and June 19th, and is linked to the planet Mars.

West: Silver Birch

Silver Birch is a feminine tree corresponding to the element of water and known as, "The Lady of the Woods." The Silver Birch is invoked for new beginnings and has an ability to seed itself quickly on newly cleared land. The White Peak district of Derbyshire is very conducive to the Silver Birch trees, and although Silver Birches have inhabited the peaks ever since the glaciers receded, the copses and woods around the stone circle of Stanton Moor are fairly modern, grown in the 19th and 20th centuries. They grow and propagate quickly, and live about ninety years, so bringing a youthful energy to the ritual. The word "Birch", or "Birks" means "bright or shining" and it relates to the first moon of the Roman calendar, between December 24th and January 21st. They are linked to the Sun, and Venus.

North: Ivy

Ivy is a feminine tree corresponding to the element of earth. It is common to Britain, climbing over buildings, walls, and up trees. It gives ground cover in areas of shade where other plants will not grow. Ivy is linked to strength of the ego and gives protection from Evil. "Gort" was the name for Ivy and it was thought to be good for re-birth, fertility, fidelity and the tenaciousness needed to complete projects. Ivy relates to the eleventh moon of the Roman calendar year, between September 30th and October 27th. It is linked to the Sun and Jupiter.

Libation:

Cakes and Ale

THE RITUAL

1. Set up the altar with the daffodils placed centrally, the rock salt and the moon and sun water to the left, and the incense and yellow candle to the right. Use tree leaves, twigs and buds, flower buds, fresh herbs and yellow crystals to decorate.

2. Place the circular dish, compost, seeds, and nine quartz crystals beside the altar.

3. To mark the Four Directions, place the bundle of Hazel to the East, Hawthorn to the South, Silver Birch to the West and Ivy to the North.

3. Cast the Circle.

4. Call in the Four Directions:

   Face the East: "I call in the Spirit of the Hazel for communication and insight. Bring the fresh wind from the East. Hail and welcome."

   Face the South: "I call in the Spirit of the Hawthorn for protection. Bring clear insight to this project. Bring fire from the South; the heat that is hotter than from all other woods. Hail and welcome."

   Face the West: "I call in the Spirit of the Silver Birch, for new beginnings and a youthful, fresh approach. Bring the refreshing element of water from the West. Hail and welcome."

   Face the North: "I call in the Spirit of the Ivy, for tenacity, strength of will and growth. Bring the grounding earthiness of the North to this ritual. Hail and welcome."

5. Sprinkle a very little salt in the sun and moon water. "I purify this water with the element of earth. I bring earth and water to this ritual. Blessed be."

6. Light the incense. "I bring the element of air to this ritual. Blessed be."

7. Light the yellow candle. "I bring the element of fire to this ritual. Blessed be."

8. Call in the Goddess Arnemetia:

"I call in the Goddess Arnemetia, Lady who lives by the Sacred Grove, please be welcome in this circle. I ask your loving blessing on this ritual. May it be for the highest good of all. Hail and welcome!"

9. State the purpose of the ritual: "This ritual is to bring vibrant new, creative energy to activate my new project (name it). May the seeds of the project be sown in fertile soil, may it be watered with life giving energy, and flourish, so that it bears fruit."

10. Raise energy by walking nine times round the circle chanting:

> *"Arnemetia of the Sacred Grove,*
> *Bring your blessing to this new birth,*
> *By hazel and hawthorn, birch and ivy*
> *By air and fire, water and earth."*

Feel the energy build up, the expectation of a good result strengthen, and the power of the Goddess become manifest.

11. Settle in front of the altar and pick up the compost. Dedicate it through the elements one by one. "I dedicate this compost to Arnemetia, through earth (sprinkle with a few grains of salt), water (sprinkle with water), air (move through the incense) and fire (move over the top of the candle). Blessed be." Place the compost in the dish.

Dedicate the nine crystals to Arnemetia, and through the elements in the same way. Place vertically in a circle round the edge of the dish, pointing downwards into the soil.

Dedicate the seeds to Arnemetia, and through the elements. Sprinkle them on the compost, according to the packet instructions.

Water with the moon and sun water.

Dedicate the finished crystal circle to Arnemetia, through the elements and state the affirmation: "My new project is conceived, rooted, and grows fruitfully." Hold up the crystal circle, and release the power of the energy raised.

12. Take time to ground yourself. Now is the time to eat the cakes and drink the ale, reserving some for Arnemetia. This can be laid outside after closing the circle.

13. Give thanks and say farewell to the Goddess:

    "Lady Arnemetia, Goddess of the Sacred Grove, I thank you for being part of this ritual and bestowing your blessing on my new project. Go if you must, stay if you will. Hail and farewell." Put out the yellow candle.

14. Give thanks and say farewell to the Tree spirits:

    Move to the North: "Spirit of the Ivy, of the Earth and the North, thank you for being part of this ritual and blessing my new project. Go if you must, stay if you will. Hail and farewell."

    Move to the West: "Spirit of the Silver Birch, of the Water and the West, thank you for being part of this ritual and blessing my new project. Go if you must, stay if you will. Hail and farewell."

    Move to the South: "Spirit of the Hawthorn, of the Fire and the South, thank you for being part of this ritual and blessing my new project. Go if you must, stay if you will. Hail and farewell."

    Move to the East: "Spirit of the Hazel, of the Air and the East, thank you for being part of this ritual and blessing my new project. Go if you must, stay if you will. Hail and farewell."

15. Walk round the circle fluffing up the boundary and restoring the space to the physical realm.

16. Place the libation outside.

17. Leave the seeds to germinate in a shaded, warm area, and keep moist. The sun and moon water can be drunk or poured out as a libation. It will not keep for more than twelve hours in the refrigerator. Don't use refrigerator-cold water on germinating seeds. When the seeds germinate and start to grow, place in a light, warm area, and keep watered. Good luck with your project!

WHAT TO DO NEXT

Action is needed, even though the ritual has taken place. Work out your action plan, set times for achievements, and seek advice where necessary. The positive energies invoked during the ritual will speed your actions on their way and smooth the path.

MEDITATION

Close your eyes and relax. Breathe deeply in, allowing the air to be drawn right down to your belly. Then let it go very slowly and gently. Repeat this twice more.

Create a protective bubble of white light around yourself. This is a secure place to which you can return at any time. Hold the image in your mind. You are sitting in the very centre, surrounded by white light. This will not let anything harm you. You are protected and safe.

You notice a stream of bright light streaming into your safe place. Gradually the sunlight fills your safe place and you are enveloped in glorious, warm sunshine.

As your eyes adjust to the brightness you see a moorland of heather and limestone boulders surrounding you. A well-worn track leads towards some silver birch trees in the distance. Follow the path.

Enjoy the spring sunshine and early flowers pushing between tufts of coarse grasses. The path leads into woodland of silver birch trees edged with hawthorn and hazels. The floor of the wood is carpeted with last year's fallen leaves that rustle beneath your feet. Bluebells and wild garlic grow fresh, new leaves, and ivy twines and curls its way round the roots of the trees.

You arrive at an area of open ground, an arena of grassland within the wood. A stone circle stands in the centre of this grassy area. Nearby two tall standing stones are positioned apart from the stone circle.

Walk to the stone circle. It is late morning and the shadows, cast by yourself and the stones, are short and lie to the West.

Enter the circle from the East, feeling the sun's warmth on your back and following your shadow into the circle. Look around the stone circle, turning clockwise, and notice the character of each stone. Some are tall, others wide, some worn and smooth, some rugged, grey and silver lichen grows on the limestone. Count nine stones.

Feel the ancientness of the circle. Let the circle take you back, back in time, back to the beginning. As you turn clockwise round the circle, turn within into your own power. Now, lay your creative project in the centre of the circle, the creation that you are ready to nurture from seed to harvest, breathe life into, birth into being and grow to completion. As you lay it down, the sun moves directly overhead. It is noon and shadows disappear. You hear the sound of pipers playing an ethereal dance tune, an enchanting, wild and beautiful melody.

Round you, nine ladies dance, swirling mist-grey dresses light as gossamer, translucent silver through which white-gold sunbeams shine.

They circle, weaving their dance around you. The music is getting faster. Feel the exuberance and enjoyment within the circle. The ladies smile, stepping lightly, turning and twisting. Dance with them. You feel lifted above the cares of the world, with all its fretfulness and problems, and you are filled with energy as life-giving as the sunlight beaming down on you as you dance around, through, in and out, caught up in the pipers' tune.

Now the music slows and fades and you move back to the centre of the circle, watching your shadow forming to the East, growing longer little by little. You see the circle's stones once again; the nine dancing ladies have moved within.

Take the knowledge that your creation has received a blessing from the nine ladies of the stones and its "dance" has started.

In your pocket you have nine quartz crystal points. Starting in the East, walk anticlockwise around the circle leaving a quartz point at the foot of each stone as a thanksgiving. When you reach East again, leave the circle.

Walk over the grass to the two tall standing stones, the Pipers. Feel the cool, rough stone under your fingers. Move between the two stones and find yourself back in your safe place.

Sit in your safe place.

Breathe in peace, and release

Breathe in joy, and release

Breathe in love, and release

When you are ready, open your eyes.

You are back. Welcome home.

Verbeia

On the high moor
Sheltered by rowan
Shadowed by crags,
Look down on the serpent goddess.
Curvaceous, sinuous,
Gliding over rock,
Twisting round stone,
Carving her path,
Eroding edges,
Reforming, transforming,
Whirlpools and waterfalls,
Dance of foam and stone,
Forked tongue flicks,
Teasing soil from roots,
Exposing bones,
Descending across an ancient land.

Ritual for Problem Solving Obstructions and Blockages

Verbeia: she who bends and turns

Goddess of the River Wharfe, Yorkshire

PURPOSE

To work around blockages to enable the project to go forward, or a problem to be solved.

AIM

To form a model from clay, depicting Bronze Age cup and ring marks, Celtic abstract patterns, spirals and swirls, symbolising the flow of water as it moves round rocks and flows in different directions.

AFFIRMATION

The energy flows round obstructions, and finds its own path, bringing forward movement.

TIME

The Spring, April. The Roman word "Ver," is the root of words such as "Vernal" (Spring), "Verdant" (green), and "Vernatio" (the flourishing renewal of plants in spring).

THE GODDESS

Verbeia, Goddess of the River Wharfe, is documented on an inscribed stone found under a set of steps in Ilkley by William Camden, a visitor to Ilkley, in 1528. The inscription,

> Verbiae
> Sacrum
> Clodius
> Fronto
> D
> Praef. Coh
> II Lingon

is commonly translated as:

> "To holy Verbeia, Clodius Fronto, prefect of the Second Cohort of Lingones (dedicated this)."

The inscription itself, is a tenuous connection to a Roman soldier's beliefs and gratitude to what may be a Genius Loci of the local area. But Verbeia becomes more significant when it is understood that the Roman Cohort stationed in the fort at the present day site of Ilkley, were

Gauls from the Lingones tribe in Northern Italy. Their homeland was the province Cisalpine Gaul, within which was the town of Mavilly. The infantry based in Ilkley may have brought their own local Goddess with them, and assimilated her with the water goddess of the River Wharfe, worshipped by the local people.

Another altar stone can be found in All Saints Parish Church, Ilkley. It shows a woman, wearing pleated skirts and a headdress, and holding two snakes, one in each hand. The two snakes converge at the hip. In Mavilly, a plaque of a woman in a pleated skirt holding two snakes in one hand, has been found. Is she the same Goddess, transported from Mavilly and replanted in West Yorkshire? Is this the "Verbeia" mentioned by Claudio Fronto? For the purpose of this ritual, we will accept this as possible.

From folk tales from the area around Ilkley, we know that the Goddess of the notoriously dangerous Strid, a fast flowing channel between vertical rock walls found higher up the Wharfe, manifests as a White Horse, just before she claims a victim. The Goddess of the Wharfe is wild and dangerous, as well as nurturing and life-giving.

SUBJECT: OBSTRUCTIONS

An obstruction may be a problem to be solved, a difficulty to be accommodated, a challenge to be overcome, or a lesson to be learned. If we meet obstructions head on we often find they are immovable. However, if we see obstructions as a warning to be heeded, or subject for investigation before proceeding, then we can learn much and often overcome it. Look for ways round problems, and try to find solutions. An obstruction does not mean we cannot achieve something, but it does mean we may have to work hard to find a way round it. Take a lesson from the flow of water, which does not try to move the obstruction (although the sheer force of water may sometimes do just that), but flows around and creates alternative pathways.

CORRESPONDENCES

THE RIVER WHARFE

The name Wharfe suggests a whirling, twisting vortex, changing and flowing, turning and circling, as the water and rocks create rapids. In the Indo-European language of the Celtic migrating tribes of Europe, "wert" means to turn, in the context of "to turn into", or "become". Similarly, in Middle English, "hwerfen" means to change and Simeon of Durham writes, "Hwerver" and "Hwerf" in the same context. Ormin, in the 12th Century AD, spells "hwerfen" as "wharfen" and here we see the root of the name of the River Wharfe. This is supported by Scandanavian words such as "hvarf" and "hverfi" meaning a bend or a corner. The River Wharfe is constantly changing depending on the weather, the amount of water descending from the Pennines and the season of the year.

ROCK ART

Cup marks and engraved circles are found on rocks all over Rombald's Moor on the slopes behind St Mary's Church, in Ilkley. These date from the Stone Age (Neolithic, 5000-2000 BC) to the late Iron Age (500 BC). The "Badger Stone" and the "Panorama Stone" are excellent examples. The cup and ring markings are almost always on horizontal planes, suggesting that the natural filling of the cups with rainwater may be important. It is also noticeable that they dominate the north side of the moor, where there is a view point that overlooks the river. The frequency of examples of rock art is greater nearer springs and streams.

SNAKES

The two snakes, held by the woman, converge around her hips. These may represent the two streams that flow down from Rombald's

Moor either side of the Roman Fort where her altar once stood, into the River Wharfe. The same symbolism, however, is seen on other examples of artwork such as the relief from Mavilly—Mandelot in France, the "Snake-witch Stone" from Smiss near Gotland in Sweden, and the Snake Goddess from Crete.

EQUIPMENT

The Altar:
> A symbol of Verbeia, a small figurine holding two snakes : a drawing or clay model prepared earlier
> Stones for the altar and marking the edge of the circle

The Elements:
> Air: an essential oil diffuser and essential oils with earth and herbal notes
> Fire: blue candle
> Water: water in a dish
> Earth: rock salt on a dish

Ritual Items:
> Air dry clay or flour-salt dough
> Clay moulding tools, pointed sticks, cocktail stick, pencil
> Board or plate on which to place the clay and present it
> Matches

Libation:
> Cakes and Ale

The Four Directions:
> Draw the following shapes on four pieces of paper and place each symbol at the relevant compass point on the perimeter of the circle. These symbols are reminiscent of the rock art glyphs of Rombald's Moor, Ilkley.

East: an upward curving arc

South: a circle

West: a downward curving arc

North: a spiral

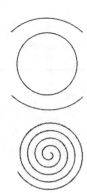

THE RITUAL

1. Set up the altar, and place the ritual items next to it.
2. Set the four rock art symbols at each of the four directions.
3. Cast the Circle.
4. Call in the Four Directions:

    Face the East: "I call in the Spirit of East, the rising sun, and the early morning light that reflects on the river. Bring the element of air from the East. (Make the sign already drawn, in the air over the compass point East.) Hail and welcome."

    Face the South: "I call in the Spirit of South, the noon-day sun, the overhead light that shines brightly on the river. Bring the element of fire from the South. (Make the sign already drawn, in the air over the compass point South.) Hail and welcome."

    Face the West: "I call in the Spirit of the West, the disappearing sun, the dimming light that brings soft shadows to the river. Bring the element of water from the West. (Make the sign already drawn, in the air over the compass point West.) Hail and welcome."

    Face the North: "I call in the Spirit of the North, the darkness of night, and the reflected moonshine on the river. Bring the element of earth from the North. (Make the sign already drawn, in the air over the compass point North.) Hail and welcome."

5. Sprinkle a little rock salt in the water. "I purify this water with the element of earth. I bring earth and water to this ritual. Blessed be."

6. Light the incense. "I bring the element of air to this ritual. Blessed be."

7. Light the blue candle. "I bring the element of fire to this ritual. Blessed be."

8. Call in the Goddess Verbeia:

    "I call in the Goddess Vebeia, Lady of the River Wharfe, she who bends and turns, please be welcome in this circle. I ask your loving blessing on this ritual. May it be for the highest good of all. Hail and welcome!"

9. State the purpose:

    "This ritual is to remove or accommodate blockages or obstructions, and enable the project to go forward, and the problem to be solved."

10. Raise energy in the circle. Use clockwise movement round the circle, dance or walk your own "cup," "circle" or "spiral".

    Chant:

    "Lady Verbeia,
    Twisting and turning,
    Whirling and bending,
    Circling round.
    Goddess of stone,
    Water hewn boulders,
    Spiralling, wheeling,
    Bring blessing now."

    Feel the energy build up, the expectation of a good result strengthen, and the power of the Goddess become manifest.

11. Settle in front of the altar and pick up the clay and the tools. Wet it with the water from the altar if necessary. Shape it into a rough boulder with a fairly flat top surface.

Make your own cup marks and rings on the clay. Draw patterns, mould cups, create circles round the cups, link them and overlay them. As you do it, see the fluidity of the circle, think of the fluidity of water on stone, water on clay, the flow of the River Wharfe round stones, moulding, eroding, moving them. Think of water flowing round stones and moving on regardless, the flexibility of water, the flexibility of clay, the water within the clay, the markings that can be erased, remarked, and the clay that can be remoulded. See the problem or blockage being changed. Finish by creating a pattern that means something to you: it may be abstract and relate to your subconscious, or it may be consciously understandable. It may be symmetrical and ordered, or natural, flowing and irregular.

Dedicate the clay to Verbeia:

"Lady of the twisting, turning, bending river,
Lady of change and transformation,
Lady of the whirlpools, and the spiralling circles of life,
Lady of the River Wharfe,
I offer you this clay as a symbol of creating a fresh approach
to the problem, flow around the blockages and bring
resolution to the situation.
By Water and Earth, Air and Fire,
I ask your blessing on this, for the highest good.
So mote it be."

The clay is earth, and contains water. Move it through the incense to dedicate it to air, and move it through the blue candle flame to dedicate it to fire. Air and warmth will dry the clay pattern.

Release the energy of the circle by dancing or walking the spiral outwards.

12. Take time to ground yourself. Now is the time to eat the cakes and drink the ale, reserving some for Verbeia. This can be laid

outside after closing the circle. The clay can be also be a libation to the Goddess, as it is a natural organic product.

13. Give thanks and say farewell to the Goddess:

"Lady Verbeia, Goddess of the River Wharfe, I thank you for being part of this ritual and bestowing your blessing on my new project. Go if you must, stay if you will. Hail and farewell." Put out the blue candle.

14. Give thanks and say farewell to the Spirits of the Four Directions.

Move to the North: "Spirit of the North and the Earth, the darkness of night, and the reflected moonshine on the river, thank you for being part of this ritual and bringing your blessing. Go if you must, stay if you will. Hail and farewell."

Move to the West: "Spirit of the West and Water, the disappearing sun, the dimming light that brings soft shades to the river, thank you for being part of this ritual and bringing your blessing. Go if you must, stay if you will. Hail and farewell."

Move to the South: "Spirit of the South and Fire, the noon-day sun and the overhead light that shines brightly on the river, thank you for being part of this ritual and bringing your blessing. Go if you must, stay if you will. Hail and farewell."

Move to the East: "Spirit of the East and Air, the rising sun, and the early morning light that reflects on the river, thank you for being part of this ritual and bringing your blessing. Go if you must, stay if you will. Hail and farewell."

15. Walk round the circle fluffing up the boundary and restoring the space to the physical realm.

16. Place the libation outside.

17. Leave the clay to dry. If it is flour and salt dough, then bake it on a very low heat in the oven for several hours. When dry it can be painted and varnished. Or it could be sent back to the elements by placing it on the earth to return to the earth.

WHAT TO DO NEXT

The energy raised in the ritual, and the blessing received must be used to keep the project from stagnating. The problems must still be solved, but the ritual will open up new possibilities and the willingness to consider them. Keep an open mind, and try new ways of thinking and acting.

MEDITATION

Close your eyes and relax. Breathe deeply in, allowing the air to be drawn right down to your belly. Then let it go very slowly and gently. Repeat this twice more.

Create a protective bubble of white light around yourself. This is a secure place to which you can return at any time. Hold the image in your mind. You are sitting in the very centre, surrounded by white light. This will not let anything harm you. You are protected and safe.

Sitting in your safe place, become aware that the boundaries of your safe place have faded and you can see that you are situated in moorland, surrounded by heather and rocky crags. A honey scented breeze wraps round you. Listen to the busy hum of insects and the call of moorland birds.

Down the hillside is a valley of green fields, trees, dry stone walls and far away, some houses. The River Wharfe twists and curves between tree lined banks.

Follow a clear path down from the moor and walk between sycamore, beech, hazel and hawthorn to the river's edge. Much of the river is tumbled with rocks, but pools of deeper water have formed between larger rock formations. The water flows purposefully on its route to the sea.

Look at the river with its tossing waters and tumbling rapids. Foam churns around the rocks, boulders, tree roots and branches. As you watch the light glinting on the surface, you see the shape of a woman amongst the turning whirls of water. She seems to beckon, smiling and waving. Sense her enjoyment and exhilaration. Reach your arms into the cool water and feel the tug of the current. Let go of your physical body and leave it on the riverbank. Allow Verbeia to pull you into the water.

You are caught in a whirling torrent of churning water, but feel no fear. Ride with it. It is full of energy, swirling, coursing round rocks, spraying over stones, curving round boulders. Tumble with it, laughing, gleeful, riding the waves and whirled round in a dance.

Merge with the water and become one with its motion, movement and energy. Your restrictions and confines have gone. You are free. Nothing holds you back. The water flows with wild abandonment and so do you. Round, up, down, over, it surges.

Flow down shallow rapids and find yourself in deeper water: a calm pool. Looking up through the water you see your physical body standing on stepping stones that cross the river. As you reach up through the surface of the water, your body reaches down and you become one.

Back in your body you feel the sunlight warming you, and smell the damp earth of the river bank. Look into the river and see Verbeia swimming in a spiral counter-clockwise, and descending to the depths. She disappears from sight.

You know that whatever problems, restrictions and seemingly insurmountable blockages there are in your life, you will find ways to flow round, up, down, and over them.

Now you see a beautiful piece of beech tree bark curved like a boat lying next to the stepping stones. Hold it in your cupped hands and fill it with thanksgiving for Verbeia. Float it on the water and watch as the current gently carries it away, downstream.

Turn from the river and follow a broad, grassy track away through the trees and onto the grassland. Follow it between two dry stone walls. See some heather growing by the wall and pick a little to take with you. In the distance, higher up the moor, there is a small stone cottage, with an open doorway. This intrigues you, so walk up to the cottage and through the open doorway. You are back in your safe place. Sit or lie in your safe place and hold your heather.

Breathe in peace, and release

Breathe in joy, and release

Breathe in love, and release
You are ready to open your eyes.
You are back. Welcome home.

Belisama

There are flames on the water tonight
The descending sun, the darkening sky
A funeral pyre, balanced momentarily
On the world's watery edge.
One last backward glance, then it slips
Softly, unnoticeably, over the horizon,
Leaving dark on dark, diffusing, deceiving,
Sky and water, merging.
I cannot tell you when it ceased
To ride the waves.

An ochre pathway trails
Across indigo waves.
Dragon's breath licks the sea's surface
Flickering bewitchingly, beckoning enticingly,
"Come beloved, follow Belisama."

I step onto the gold-gleaming sweep,
The shock of cold, claws my soul,
The tug of the tide: inhale, exhale, inhale.
Seaweed tendrils clasp my knees,
Mermaids' hair entwines my waist,
I succumb to their hypnotic song,
Numbing heart and mind,
A golden net spills ocean wide,
Capturing the entranced.

Enraptured, I am driven from glory to glory,
Ride the flaming solar chariot,
Rage the blackened skies,
The diamond studded darkness,
Flames carve our path,
Pulled by lightening,
Thunder crushing,
Bel whips her frenzied fiery steeds,
On and on.

The virgin dawn rises pink and tearful
Through silver cumulous clouds,
A gentle breeze inhales, exhales
Shoes lie empty on a tide washed beach.

Ritual for Relinquishing Negativity whilst Retaining the Positive

Belisama: "Summer Bright,"
She who purifies by fire

Solar Goddess of the River Ribble, Lancashire

PURPOSE

To rid oneself of the negative aspects of a situation, whilst retaining and strengthening the positive.

AIM

To separate the negative and positive aspects of a situation. These aspects are written down on separate slips of paper and the negative aspects are burnt in a black candle's flame to release it for transmutation. The positive aspects are burnt in a white candle's flame, and the Goddess Belisama is called upon to strengthen resolve, and bring healing and guidance.

AFFIRMATION

I hold goodness within me.

TIME

Beltane, May 1st

THE GODDESS

Belisama's presence has been traced back to Romano-Gaulish inscriptions found throughout France, including one such inscription at Vaison-la-Romaine in Provence-Alpes-Cotes D'Azur. The Vocontii settled here in the 4th century BC. By 20 AD it had become a Roman Colony and was named Vasio Vocontiorum, the remains of which can be seen today, situated on the right bank of the River Ouveze. The Romans equated this Gaulish Goddess with their own Minerva, and re-named her Minervae Belissimae. She made her way to Great Britain with the migration of the Gauls and the invasion of the Romans, and it is thought that the River Ribble (*Belisama Fluvius*) was named after her.

On his map of Northern Britain, Ptolemy named the estuary of a river north of Chester, Belisama Aest, and although this was initially thought to be the River Mersey, this has now been discounted and is understood to be the River Ribble. The River Ribble's estuary meets the sea between Lytham St Annes and Southport in Lancashire, but the source is found at the confluence of Gayle Beck and Cam Beck at Ribblehead, in Yorkshire. The River Ribble was guarded by a garrison at Ribchester (*Bremetenacvm Veteranorvm*, "The Hilltop Settlement of the Veterans") in AD1. The Roman Fort soon developed a thriving civilian settlement. However the lands surrounding Ribchester were given to the Roman Veterans, and these had previously belonged to the people of the Brigantes. Several inscriptions were found in Ribchester, on altars dedicated to Mars, Apollo and the Goddess Victory. However, none have been found dedicated to Belisama.

In France, the country then known as Gaul, Belisama was the female consort of the God Belenus, a sun God of healing, who was integrated by the Romans with the God Apollo. Belisama was worshipped as a summer solar Goddess. In Proto-celtic "belo" is interpreted as "bright" and "samo" as "summer", therefore her name may mean "Summer Bright".

Belenus and Belisama are traditionally invoked at the May festival of Beltane. Two fires of purification were lit and the cattle that had wintered in the low pastures were driven between the fires, so that the smoke from the fires purified them before they moved to the summer pastures. We take the essence of this concept for our ritual.

SUBJECT: DIFFICULT SITUATIONS

Many times in our lives we find ourselves in situations, often of our own making, that are extremely difficult. We may feel trapped, or we may be able to change that situation by making tough decisions. Just as the skilfully wielded surgeon's scalpel cuts away diseased tissue allowing new growth, we too need to cut away the cankerous growths in our lives that are doing us no good.

However, one of the difficulties of doing this is that it is rarely as simple as ridding ourselves of negative aspects of a situation. Within the situation there is much good. There are qualities in ourselves that are raised up and these should not be lost. The ritual is designed to help us cut away and rid ourselves of the negative, whilst retaining and honouring, accepting and nourishing that which is beneficial to us.

This ritual is not necessarily about endings, but is definitely about transformation.

CORRESPONDENCES

THE RIVER RIBBLE

The head of the River Ribble, *Belisama Fluvis,* rises as a tiny spring in North Yorkshire near the peaks of Ingleborough, Whernside and Penyghent. The Ribble flows down the Pennines, through Lancashire to become an estuary between Lytham St Annes and Southport.

What was thought to be an Iron Age hillfort can be seen today on the top of Ingleborough, and another can be found at Castercliff. Clam Bridge at Wycoller in Pendle dates to the Iron Age. The bridge is a single slab of stone laid across the beck. Iron Age brooches, carvings and a Bronze Age sword have been found in the area, and are located in Ribchester Museum.

The Romans built a fort to guard the Ribble at Ribchester in Lancashire. Bremetenacvm Veteranorvm was established in AD1, and later it developed into a civilian settlement. It has been suggested that Roman veterans lived here and were provided with land that had been inhabited by the Brigantes. The name Ribchester originates from Ribelcastre, "Roman Fort on the River Ribble". Another Roman fort was built at Kirkham and linked by road to Ribchester.

FIRE

The element of fire is masculine and associated with Summer, the Sun and transmutation. Fire can be very dangerous and destructive, but it can also purify, cleanse and warm.

WHITE AND RED COLOURS

Traditionally, white and red colours were the colours of the ribbons that hung on the maypole. The ribbons were the feminine aspect of the maypole, and the central pole was the masculine aspect. White and red ribbons are used at handfastings to bind the hands of the man and woman who are celebrating their union.

PURIFICATION BY SMOKE

Smudging originates in the Native American Indian tradition, where herbs are used to cleanse the aura of negative energy. Loose leaves of white sage are burnt slowly in an abalone shell and wafted into the aura of a person using a feather. Smudge sticks are herbs that have been bound in bundles for ease of use. Native American Indians invoke the Spirit of the herb to do the actual cleansing.

EQUIPMENT

The Altar:
>   Symbol for the Goddess: a pure white, large candle. Chose a spherical
>   candle or one that symbolises the Divine Feminine by shape
>   Altar cloths in red and white
>   Flowers and foliage

The Elements:
>   Air: White Sage smudging leaves
>   Fire: a fire pit, barbeque or portable tin-foil barbeque, charcoal
>   Water: water in a bowl
>   Earth: rock salt on a dish

Ritual Items:
>   A black candle
>   A white candle

Matches
Slips of paper
A pen
A drum, or use hands to clap
For safety: a fire extinguisher or fire blanket

Libation:
Food to cook on the barbeque and bread
Mead, wine or ale

The Four Directions:
Four tea lights in four lanterns

THE RITUAL

Ideally this ritual will be held outside, and this means that a wind-free area needs to be found. Otherwise, keep candles in lanterns and create a wind break. Be aware of the danger of candles and fire, and never leave them unattended.

1. Set up the altar, and place the ritual items next to it.
2. Set the four tea light lanterns at each of the four directions.
3. Cast the Circle.
4. Call in the Four Directions:
   Face the East:
   "I call in the Spirit of the Guardian of the East, of Air, the Sunrise, and the Spring. Hail and welcome." Light the lantern.
   Face the South:
   "I call in the Spirit of the Guardian of the South, of Fire, the Noon, and the Summer. Hail and welcome." Light the lantern.
   Face the West:

"I call in the Spirit of the Guardian of the West, of Water, the Setting Sun, and the Autumn. Hail and welcome." Light the lantern.

Face the North:

"I call in the Spirit of the Guardian of the North, of Earth, Midnight, and the Winter. Hail and welcome." Light the lantern.

5. Light the fire pit or barbeque. "I bring the element of fire to this ritual. Blessed be."

6. Place the smudging herbs on the barbeque. "I bring the element of air to this ritual. Blessed be."

7. Sprinkle a little salt in the water. Say, "I purify this water with the element of earth. I bring earth and water to this ritual. Blessed be."

8. Call in the Goddess:

"I call in the Goddess Belisama, please be welcome in this circle. May this ritual of purification be for the highest good of all. Hail and welcome!" Light the white candle.

10. State the purpose of the ritual:

"This ritual is to rid myself of negativity (name your situation) and yet I recognise there is good mixed with the negative. This good, I will keep. I call on the Goddess Belisama to support me and help me."

10. State the affirmation:

"I hold goodness within me."

11. Walk the circle nine times round, clockwise, drumming a beat on the drum to raise energy and power. Raise your arms, and visualise the energy of white light from the Goddess Belisama entering your crown and pouring down through your body. It pushes all darkness away. It flows through you, around you, out through your limbs, and empowers you.

12. Settle in front of the altar and light the black candle.

Say, "This black candle burns up the negative energy released during this ritual, and transmutes it to white light. Let it benefit our planet earth."

Light the white candle. Say, "This white candle strengthens my resolve and communicates to Belisama, that there are good things I want to keep and work with to strengthen and bless me. Belisama, please help me in this."

Muse on your situation. Within the situation there are aspects you need to release. Look honestly at them, and consider these clearly. When you are ready, write down these aspects on slips of paper. Place them on a pile to one side.

Think about the same situation. Although much is wrong with it, and much needs to be changed or let go of, there are aspects that bless you, develop you, strengthen and teach you. The situation has brought some of your own gifts to the forefront. These you can keep. Write these down on slips of paper and place them on a second pile.

Take a slip, read it, think about it. If negative then burn the paper in the black candle and let the issue go.

Take another, read it, think about it. If positive then burn the paper in the white candle and ask Belisama's help in transforming it into a blessing.

You can start with all the negative issues, then move onto the positive issues, or vice versa. It may be helpful, to alternate, taking one from the negative pile, and one from the positive pile until both piles are finished.

13. Take the food you have prepared to cook and place on the barbeque. When it is ready, eat the food and drink the ale, leaving a portion of bread and ale for Belissima. This can be laid on the ground as an offering.

Enjoy your time outdoors next to the fire, in the company of Belisama. The full summer has not come yet, but is on its way. There is much to look forward to. Ponder on how you will move forward positively from this ritual while you cook, eat and drink.

14. Give thanks and say farewell to the Belisama.

"Thank you for helping me to let go of the negative aspects of this situation. Help me to do my very best with the positive aspects I have retained. Thank you. Go if you must, stay if you will. Hail and farewell." Put out her candle.

15. Give thanks and say farewell to the Guardian Spirits of the Four Directions.

Move to the North:

"Spirit of the Guardian of the North, of Earth, of Midnight, and of Winter, thank you for being in this circle and part of this ritual. Go if you must, stay if you will, hail and farewell." Put out the lantern.

Move to the West:

"Spirit of the Guardian of the West, of Water, the Setting Sun, and the Autumn, thank you for being in this circle and part of this ritual. Go if you must, stay if you will, hail and farewell." Put out the lantern.

Move to the South:

"Spirit of the Guardian of the South, of Fire, the Noon, and the Summer, thank you for being in this circle and part of this ritual. Go if you must, stay if you will, hail and farewell." Put out the lantern.

Move to the East:

"Spirit of the Guardian of the East, of Air, the Sunrise, and the Spring, thank you for being in this circle and part of this ritual. Go if you must, stay if you will, hail and farewell." Put out the lantern.

16. Raise your hand to the circle edge, fluffing up the boundary and restoring the space to the physical realm.

17. Place the libation in a suitable place. Cooked food should be disposed of carefully. Ensure the fire pit and the black and white candles are extinguished.

WHAT TO DO NEXT

Do not hold onto that which is wrong within the situation. Let it go once and for all and accept the reality of the situation. This may mean taking time to hold difficult meetings to communicate difficult messages. Hold strongly to what you know is best for you. Take the positive aspects of your situation forward and see how you can build on them. This may take time, especially in circumstances concerning relationships. But over time, see what you can salvage. Something must be cut away, but this does not mean that everything has to be lost. Seek advice and always weigh that advice to see if it is the right advice for you. Go forwards, and don't look back.

MEDITATION

Close your eyes and relax. Breathe deeply in, allowing the air to be drawn right down to your belly. Then let it go very slowly and gently. Repeat this twice more.

Create a protective bubble of white light around yourself. This is a secure place to which you can return at any time. Hold the image in your mind. You are sitting in the very centre, surrounded by white light. This will not let anything harm you. You are protected and safe.

Your safe place shapes itself into a cottage kitchen. There is a fire burning in the stone hearth, herbs hang drying from the ceiling. You are sitting on a wooden chair on a stone flagged floor. Through an open door smell a waft of wood smoke and wonder where it comes from. You see the wooden door is open. Stand and walk to the door.

Across the green field you see a large bonfire. Walk across the field. Underfoot is coarse green grass, red and white clover and some daisies. You walk easily across the field. High in the sky the sun's fiery light causes short shadows to follow you. It is nearly noon.

As you walk closer to the May Day bonfire you realise how big the fire is. The flames are taking hold of tree branches and rise to the sky. Feel the heat burning down on you. Next to the fire are two wood piles.

One pile is heaped with white silver birch branches, and the other with blackthorn branches. They are ready to be placed on the fire.

Watch the fire for a while.

Feel the heat.

Hear the crackle as sticks burn.

See the flames: purple, yellow, orange.

Smell the smoke as the light breeze drifts it around you.

Let the smoke cleanse and purify your aura. Welcome it.

You stare into the heart of the fire, and see the shape of a woman emerge through the flames and burning wood. She comes towards you white hot, glowing with gold. You recognise Belisama. You feel as if you are splitting into parts—there is so much you want to release, yet so much you want to keep.

Belisama asks you what you want to release. Tell her.

She asks you to give her a black branch and you place a blackthorn branch into Belisama's left hand. As she takes it you are able to release your issue. The blackthorn branch bursts into flames in her hand and she raises it above her head as an offering to the fire. It is transformed into pure light. For a moment the sun seems to join the bonfire's flames in a column of fire and light reaching to the heavens.

You have no shadow. It is noon.

Belisama asks you what you would like to keep. You tell her.

She asks you to give her a white branch and you place a silver birch branch into Belisama's right hand. As she takes it you state that you would like to keep this issue in a way that serves your highest good. The white branch bursts into flames in her hand and she raises it above her hand as an offering to the fire. It is transformed into pure light.

Feel the sun's rays on the crown of your head, and a surge of warmth coursing through your body, balancing and energising you.

You thank Belisama and she smiles. Then she merges with the flames and becomes part of the heart of the fire once more.

Watch the flames a little longer.

Turn and walk across the field towards the small stone cottage in the corner of the field. The wooden door is open.

Walk inside and find yourself in your safe place. Sit down on the wooden chair by the kitchen fire and relax.

Take a deep breath and release it.

Take another deep breath and release it.

Take a third deep breath and release it.

When you are ready open your eyes. Welcome back.

Su-lījīs

From the darkness flows the water,
Fresh from the earthen otherworld,
Between the parting of the rocks,
The Suil.

Explore the orifice, rock on rock,
Press my fingers against the lip
Palm to palm with her hand,
Link fingers.

I am pulled against the flow,
The Suil encloses me,
Darkness and water wrap round.

Curl inwards,
Abandon all desires,
Discover my small self,
Be, only be.

Her arms support me,
Lift me beyond all I ever was,
Make me.

From the darkness flows the water,
Carries me into sunlight,
Mist parts, revealing
All that is new.

Ritual to Set Right a Situation

Su-lijis: "Good Flooding One,"
She who sets things right

Goddess of the thermal waters of Bath

PURPOSE

To set right that which is wrong in your life.

AIM

To skry using melted candle wax and water, "see" into situations to reveal information, and use this information to set this right.

AFFIRMATION

I live righteously, in truth, and I forgive.

TIME

Summer Solstice, 21st June.

THE GODDESS

Su-lijis is understood to be a Proto-Celtic name meaning "Good Flooding One". The thermal waters that flowed through the opening were considered mystical, pouring from the Otherworld into our world through the "suil," the orifice, eye or gap. It may have been that Su-lijis guarded the gateway between realms. It is also possible that Su-lijis may have been linked to the Norse Sun Goddess Sól.

The Romans adopted the Goddess and Latinized her name, whereby she became known as Sulis, both Sun Goddess and Goddess of the natural thermal springs of Bath. They named the town Aquae Sulis and, as was often their way, they synthesised the Genius Loci with their own Goddess, Minerva, resulting in worship of Sulis-Minerva. Whereas references to Minerva can be found throughout Europe, Sulis Minerva's name was only found on inscriptions in the locality of Bath.

In both Aquae Sulis and Aquae Arnemetia (Buxton, Derbyshire) the Romans built spa baths harnessing the warm waters that flow from the underground springs. The springs still pump water at 46° Celsius into the Roman Baths and can be experienced in the modern Thermae Spa today.

The Geni Loci of the Celtic people were approached with similar requests wherever they were located. They were invoked by Romans and Britons to bring justice, correct wrong doing, stop theft, grant healing, bear witness to oaths, ensure the safe passage of childbirth and death, and recover lost items. Thus, they were requested to support the ordinary day-to-day life of the common people.

In our ritual we invoke Sul-lijis to help us understand everyday situations, behaviour, words and to enable us to unravel problems in a similar way to our Celtic predecessors.

SUBJECT: RIGHTEOUSNESS

Sometimes we feel we are right, and we know we are right, but every person has a different viewpoint. How do we know what is "right?" We have been brought up in a particular family tradition, and our family's traditions and beliefs were instilled into us. But does this make us "right?" We live life according to what we know, but how do we know everything, and understand everything from every person's point of view? Skrying can help, because it peels back the layers of learnt behaviour, and reveals a nugget of objective truth. It is up to us to embrace this, and use it for the highest good.

CORRESPONDENCES

WATER

Thermal springs, the healing element of water warmed by fire, bubbling forth from the earth, have been used for centuries to relieve the body of illness, aches and pains. From holy wells to sacred springs, water has been recognised as life giving, healing and purifying.

THE SUN

The healing rays of the sun warm the body and provide nourishing Vitamin D. The electromagnetic energy of the Sun's rays keep life alive on Earth.

THE THRESHOLD

The Otherworld is separated from the physical world and was thought, and still is believed by many, to be accessible by seeking and finding a threshold, a door or thinly veiled boundary. The seashore, holed rocks known as "holey stones", caves, cracks and chasms in rock faces, trees, springs and wells are all used as thresholds. The veil between this life and the Otherworld is said to be at its thinnest at Samhain, October 31st to November 1st and Beltane, April 30th to May 1st. The "suil" at Bath through which the sacred spring pours is one such threshold.

SKRYING

Skrying is a form of divination. The word "skry" comes from the an older word "descry" which means to catch sight of, discern or detect that which is distant, obscured or unclear. When we skry, we tap into our unconscious and let it speak to our conscious. For many who use divination, the knowledge comes as a brief flash of inspiration, a picture in the mind's eye, or an intuitive feeling. Some people have clairvoyant gifts and "see" that which remains hidden to the rest of us.

The shape formed by wax is associated by the mind with information, pictures, concepts and ideas that are not readily available during conscious thinking, yet which are held deep within. The wax shape triggers access to those thoughts and understandings. For those who connect with Spirit, the shapes visualised open the boundaries between physical and spiritual consciousness, enabling Spirit to communicate with the skryer, and the skryer to receive and understand.

EQUIPMENT

The Altar:
> Symbol for the Goddess: a glass bowl full of spring water
> Altar cloths in colours that reflect the water element, blue, green, grey, silver

The Elements:
> Air: incense
> Fire: a gold candle
> Earth: rock salt on a dish

Ritual Items:
    Candle wax
    Double cooker (or bowl on a pan of hot water)
    Cloth for protecting hands
    Heat source
    Heat mat
    Kitchen roll absorbent paper
    Paper
    Pen

Libation:
    Cakes and ale

The Four Directions:
    East: yellow candle
    South: red candle
    West: blue candle
    North: green candle

THE RITUAL

1. Set up the altar. Place water in the base of the double cooker, or in a pan with a bowl inside. Place the candle wax inside the inner container and bring the water to the boil. At this point the candle wax should melt. Turn off the heat source. The candle wax may need another melting when you are ready to skry.
2. Set the candles at each of the four directions.
3. Cast the Circle, and include the heat source and skrying equipment within your circle if at all possible. If it is not possible, then at the appropriate point in the ritual "cut" a door in the energy circle and visualise it opening and closing as you leave the circle to complete the melting of the wax. It is important to remember to close the door after your re-entry to the circle for skrying.

4. Call in the Four Directions:
   Face the East:
   "I call in the Spirit of the Guardian of the East and of Air. Hail and welcome." Light the yellow candle.
   Face the South:
   "I call in the Spirit of the Guardian of the South and of Fire. Hail and welcome." Light the red candle.
   Face the West:
   "I call in the Spirit of the Guardian of the West and of Water. Hail and welcome." Light the blue candle.
   Face the North:
   "I call in the Spirit of the Guardian of the North and of Earth. Hail and welcome." Light the green candle.

5. Sprinkle a little salt in the water. "I purify this water with the element of earth. I bring earth and water to this ritual. Blessed be."

6. Light the incense. "I bring the element of air to this ritual. Blessed be."

7. Light the gold candle. "I bring the element of fire to this ritual. Blessed be."

9. Call in the Goddess:
   "I call in the Goddess Su-lijis, Good Flooding One, please be welcome in this circle. May it be for the highest good of all. Hail and welcome!"

10. State the purpose of the ritual: "This ritual is to bring insight and understanding into a situation to enable the setting right of the situation for the highest good."

11. Raise energy by walking nine times round the circle chanting:

"At the threshold to our world,
Where the hot springs run,
We call on you, invoke you,

Good Flooding One,
By sunlit skies, and land and stream,
Su-lijis Goddess,
Speak to me."

12. Heat the water in the double boiler or pan, re-melt the wax and bring to the altar. As you are doing so, hold your question and the situation firmly in your mind, and concentrate. Intend to gain understanding and insight into the situation.

    State the question or query out loud to Su-lijis. Drop the melted wax on the water in the bowl. Let the shapes trigger thoughts and pictures in your mind. Open your mind to allow insight to be revealed. You may wish to record your observation and received understanding.

13. State the affirmation:

    "I live righteously, in truth and I forgive."

14. Now is the time to eat the cakes and drink the ale reserving some for Su-lijis. This can be laid outside after closing the circle.

15. Give thanks and say farewell to the Su-lijis.

    "Thank you for helping me to understand new aspects of this situation. Help me to do my very best to right all wrongs, and bring healing to the situation. Thank you. Go if you must, stay if you will. Hail and farewell." Put out the gold candle.

16. Give thanks and say farewell to the Guardian Spirits of the Four Directions.

    Move to the North:

    "Spirit of the Guardian of the North and of Earth. Thank you for being in this circle and part of this ritual. Go if you must, stay if you will. Hail and farewell." Put out the green candle.

    Move to the West:

    "Spirit of the Guardian of the West and of Water. Thank you for being in this circle and part of this ritual. Go if you must, stay if you will. Hail and farewell." Put out the blue candle.

Move to the South:

"Spirit of the Guardian of the South and of Fire. Thank you for being in this circle and part of this ritual. Go if you must, stay if you will. Hail and farewell." Put out the red candle.

Move to the East:

"Spirit of the Guardian of the East and of Air. Thank you for being in this circle and part of this ritual. Go if you must, stay if you will. Hail and farewell." Put out the yellow candle.

17. Raise your hand to the circle edge, fluffing up the boundary and restoring the space to the physical realm.

18. Place the libation in a suitable place. Perhaps you will find a crevice in a rock, allow a stream to carry them off, or place in a stone with a hole in it.

WHAT TO DO NEXT

It is sometimes difficult to put situations right, especially when other people are involved. Acting as if nothing has happened is not necessarily the answer. However, neither is tackling the situation head on as the person may feel very vulnerable and criticised. They may be unaware of how you feel, or they may be harbouring hurt that they are not yet ready to relinquish. Forgiveness may be instant, when new understanding comes into the situation, but often it takes time. We are responsible for ourselves, and our own attitudes. If we put ourselves right, apologise where necessary, and act with kindness, then often as not the situation becomes something of the past and the hurts are discarded. Anguish is replaced by peace.

MEDITATION

Close your eyes and relax. Breathe deeply in, allowing the air to be drawn right down to your belly. Then let it go very slowly and gently. Repeat this twice more.

Create a protective bubble of white light around yourself. This is a secure place to which you can return at any time. Hold the image in your mind. You are sitting in the very centre, surrounded by white light. This will not let anything harm you. You are protected and safe.

Feel the drift of cool air over your face.

A rocky pool is set at the base of a hill side where flowing water has eroded away soil and left crevices and cracks visible. Water flows into this still pool through a crevice in the rock and ripples from this natural spring pattern the water. The damp rocky backdrop is overhung with small trees, ferns, grasses and red and white clovers. All is still. You feel the peace, the coolness, the gentle warmth of sunlight that filters through the trees and rests on your shoulders.

Soon shafts of golden light float down from the sun, through the tree branches, and meet the water, colouring it gold. You discern the outline of a woman, broken by ripples, yet visibly shaped on the water. She seems to be calling you.

Place your hands into the water and swirl large spirals clockwise. Then dip your feet in the water and move them back and forth. The woman's image hardly breaks; it sparkles with light. You yearn to swim, and dropping your clothing at the side of the pool, slip into the cool, refreshing waters. You are buoyant, held up in the water, and can rest.

Float, rest, and let the waters cleanse you. The waters wash away upsets, traumas, tiredness, illness, soreness, aches and pains. Let them the waters cool your mind and bring peace. Let all be still.

You feel whole, so complete. The world has been set right and you feel comfortable within it.

After a while you float to the edge of the pool. Pull yourself easily out of the pool. The sun bathes you in warmth and dries your skin. Give thanks to Su-lijis. The woman's image breaks into ripples and sparkles of sunlight and is gone.

Dress, then, as you turn away from the pool you see a path leading to a gap between the rocks. Follow the path. Walk between the rocks and find yourself in your safe place.

Sit in your safe place.

Breathe in peace, and release

Breathe in joy, and release

Breathe in love, and release

When you are ready, open your eyes.

You are back. Welcome home.

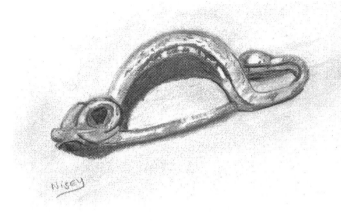

Nisey

Senua

I promise . . .
I pledge . . .
I give my word . . .

What is it I believe, so strongly, so profoundly
That I give it my power?
My spirit unifies with belief,
With faith, I bind myself,
Against logic and reason,
Understanding and certainty,
I know,
In the core of my being
Intuit,
In my soul
It is.

I promise . . .
I pledge . . .
I give my word.

Ritual to Empower a Pledge

Senua: she who helps me fulfil my pledge

Goddess of the natural spring at Ashwell, Hertfordshire

PURPOSE

To make a pledge and empower it to give you the ability to keep it.

AIM

Make a pledge and carry it out to be best of your ability. Make jewellery, dedicate it to Senua, then wear it as a reminder to keep the pledge. When the pledge is fulfilled or has become a way of life, make a votive plaque and inscribe it, stating that you have fulfilled your pledge. Then ritually break it and bury it in the earth along with the jewellery.

THE PLEDGE

I pledge to . . . .
Please note, all pledges and vows should be for the highest good of all, and harm no-one.

TIME

July or any chosen time.

THE GODDESS

Prior to 2002 the Goddess Senua was unknown and her silver statue rested, buried in the earth, along with a collection of jewellery, coins and nineteen votive plaques of gold or silver alloy. Five carried her name. A piglet and human cremated remains were buried alongside the hoard in what is now a farmer's field at Ashwell, in Hertfordshire. The statue is thought to be the Goddess Senua, deciphered from the name found inscribed on a silver statue base found adjacent to the statue. The statue is carved in Roman style, though probably by Celtic craftsmen.

On the site of the buried hoard is a natural spring, source of the River Cam. When the area was excavated, post holes were discovered suggesting that a complex of buildings surrounded the spring. This may have been an open air temple with surrounding workshops and accommodation for pilgrims. It is thought that Senua was the Goddess of the spring and the offerings were made to her for healing, requests and thanksgivings.

The jewellery was formed from wire coiled into discs and decorated with glass beads. Amongst the jewellery was a fine gold clasp set with carnelian, and engraved with a lion resting its raised paw on a bull's head.

At some point the inhabitants who lived near the spring may have been threatened and buried their offerings, jewellery, plaques and a statue in a "structured deposit" that was buried purposefully and in an orderly manner, most likely with an intention to reclaim it in safer times. It is thought that jewellery was crafted especially for gifting to the Goddess Senua.

SUBJECT: PLEDGES

When you make a pledge you need to be very serious. Do not make a pledge unless you really mean it. The Romans built altars to Gods and Goddesses and inscribed them with the words that documented that they had fulfilled their pledge. Note the start of your pledge, and the date it is finished.

CORRESPONDENCES

JEWELLERY

Iron Age jewellery was carefully crafted and beautifully made. The Brythonic craftsmen worked with bronze, iron, silver, gold and an amalgamation of silver and gold called electrum.

Torcs are nearly circular neck and arm rings made from twisted metal. For the most part they were rigid, worn with the open part at the front of the body, and because of the difficulty of removal were a nearly permanent adornment. They were worn as a status symbol by the wealthy and powerful. The Great Torc, found in the Snettisham Hoard from 1BC, was created from eight ropes of wire twisted together. Altogether one kilogram of gold mixed with silver was used. The terminal rings were richly decorated with patterns and welded to the rope ends.

The Winchester Hoard includes two torcs of different sizes, two gold brooches, and two gold bracelets. They would have been worn by people of very high status and were perhaps buried for safekeeping.

Brooches held cloaks onto the inner layers of clothing. They are often found in pairs and tend to form an early type of safety pin design. Penannular brooches were oval or circular, and a lovely example with coiled ends has been found at Marlborough. Swan Neck and Ring pins were also made to hold clothing in place, and would have been highly prized.

PLAQUES

The plaques found buried with the statue of Senua are inscribed on behalf of Roman men and women who wanted to create a record of their act of fulfilling their vow to their Goddess. They bring completion and release. This was known as an act of "Solutio".

BURYING

In the Iron Age it was common practice to bury weapons, pots, jewellery and precious items in rivers, springs, and wells as offerings to the local God or Goddess. It was also common to bend or break the item before it was buried. It is as if the mortal, physical offering that was made and used by humans, could be transformed into a spiritual item for use by the God or Goddess by bending or breaking the weapon, or smashing the pot. It also made sure that the offering would not be reclaimed for use by somebody else.

EQUIPEMENT FOR PART 1 OF THE RITUAL

The Altar:
  Symbol for the Goddess: statue made from air dried clay and painted silver
  Altar cloths in earth colours of brown, rust, and green

The Elements:
  Air: incense
  Fire: candle
  Water: a dish of natural spring water
  Earth: a dish of soil taken from the sacred, prepared ritual ground that will be used during the ritual

Ritual Items:
Jewellery making equipment such as beads, necklace thread, silver and gold coloured wire, a needle

Libation:
Cakes and ale

The Four Directions:
East: yellow candle
South: red candle
West: blue candle
North: green candle

EQUIPMENT FOR PART 2 OF THE RITUAL

The candle used in Part 1
Coins
A sheet of gold coloured paper
Pen and Ink

The Four Directions:
East: yellow candle
South: red candle
West: blue candle
North: green candle

THE RITUAL

1. Go outside and prepare a sacred place in the garden or another natural secluded place. Bless the earth and dedicate it to the Goddess Senua. "I dedicate this earth to the Goddess Senua, to become a sacred ground in which we place our offerings. Blessed be."

2. Take a little earth from this ground and place on the dish to symbolise earth on the altar.

3. Set the statue of the Goddess on the altar. Place a candle on the altar symbolising fire, incense for air, a dish of water and a dish of soil for earth

4. Set the four candles at the four quarter directions.

5. Cast the Circle.

6. Call in the Four Directions:

   Face the East: "I call in the Spirit of the Guardian of the East and the Sunrise. Hail and welcome." Light the yellow candle.

   Face the South: "I call in the Spirit of the Guardian of the South and Noon. Hail and welcome." Light the red candle.

   Face the West: "I call in the Spirit of the Guardian of the West and the Setting Sun. Hail and welcome." Light the blue candle.

   Face the North: "I call in the Spirit of the Guardian of the North and Midnight. Hail and welcome." Light the green candle.

5. Sprinkle a very little earth in the water. "I bring the elements of earth and water to this ritual. Blessed be."

6. Light the candle, and from the candle light the incense. "I bring the elements of fire and air to this ritual. Blessed be."

8. Call in the Goddess:

   "I call in the Goddess Senua of the sacred spring at Ashwell. Please be welcome in this circle. May it be for the highest good of all. Hail and welcome!" Anoint the statue with a drop of water.

9. State the purpose of the ritual: "This ritual is to make and empower my pledge."

10. State the pledge: I pledge to . . . .

11. Raise energy by walking nine times round the circle chanting:

"Senua, Senua, Senua show your face
I welcome you to this holy place

> *Goddess of the sacred spring*
> *My offerings I bring."*

Feel the energy of the Goddess Senua, draw it to yourself, contain it, hold it and give thanks.

12. Settle down by the altar. Take the fine wires, thread, gems and glass beads and use them to create a simple necklace, pendant or bracelet. As you do so, recite your pledge. Think about what you really mean by your pledge and about how you will fulfil it. When you have finished hold up your jewellery, state your pledge for the final time and dedicate the jewellery through the earth, water, air (incense) and fire (candle flame) elemental symbols on the altar. Dedicate it to Senua and ask her strength and blessing. Wear your jewellery while you fulfil your pledge or get used to the new lifestyle you have pledged to follow.

13. Now is the time to eat the cakes and drink the ale reserving some for Senua. This can be laid outside after closing the circle.

14. Give thanks and say farewell to Senua.

    "Thank you for giving me the strength and empowerment to fulfil my pledge. Help me to do my best. Thank you. Go if you must, stay if you will. Hail and farewell." Put out the candle.

15. Give thanks and say farewell to the Spirits of the Four Directions.

    Move to the North: "Spirit of the Guardian of the North and Midnight. Thank you for being part of this ritual and being a witness to my pledge. Go if you must, stay if you will. Hail and farewell." Blow out the green candle.

    Move to the West: "Spirit of the Guardian of the West and the Setting Sun. Thank you for being part of this ritual and being a witness to my pledge. Go if you must, stay if you will. Hail and farewell." Blow out the blue candle.

    Move to the South:

    "Spirit of the Guardian of the South and Noon. Thank you for being part of this ritual and being a witness to my pledge.

Go if you must, stay if you will. Hail and farewell." Blow out the red candle.

Move to the East:

"Spirit of the Guardian of the East and the Rising Sun. Thank you for being part of this ritual and being a witness to my pledge. Go if you must, stay if you will. Hail and farewell." Blow out the yellow candle.

16. Walk round the circle fluffing up the boundary and restoring the space to the physical realm.

17. Place libations outside by the Sacred Ground you prepared earlier.

WHAT TO DO NEXT

Part 2

When you have fulfilled your pledge choose a time to finish your ritual.

Cast a circle and call in Goddess Senua. Take the gold paper and pen and write on the paper an inscription, such as, "To the Goddess Senua, I have fulfilled my pledge." Sign and date it.

Take the inscription, a few coins and your jewellery outside. Dig a small hole and place the inscription and the coins in the hole. Cut the threads or wires of the jewellery and let the pieces fall into the hole. Then cover it up.

You have fulfilled your pledge.

MEDITATION

Before starting this meditation, think about an issue that you are working with. What do you need to release? What do you pledge to do to achieve an outcome? Make a note or mindfully remember this in preparation for the meditation.

Close your eyes and relax. Breathe deeply in, allowing the air to be drawn right down to your belly. Then let it go very slowly and gently. Repeat this twice more.

Create a protective bubble of white light around yourself. This is a secure place to which you can return at any time. Hold the image in your mind. You are sitting in the very centre, surrounded by white light. This will not let anything harm you. You are protected and safe.

Your safe place shapes itself into a country lane, where you find yourself standing under a group of ash trees bordering a meadow. See a pathway that leads from the trees across a meadow. The field is covered in wild summer flowers. The seed heads of the grasses are nodding in a light, warm breeze. Walk on the path to a hawthorn hedge, then follow the hedge along the edge of the field until you see a natural spring well. The fresh spring water bubbles gently into a shallow pool of clear water surrounded by rocks. Overhanging ferns, grasses, and wild flowers frame the opening of the spring. The water flows from the pool forming a infant stream that will eventually become a river.

As you look into the still waters, see your reflection looking back at you.

Call on the Goddess Senua: call three times, "Senua, Senua, Senua."

Dip your hands in the water and swirl the water anti-clockwise three times.

Now be still and release all that stops you from moving forward.

The sun shines behind you lighting your hands and warming the water. See the sunlit water cleanse your hands, and cleanse your energy.

Call on the Goddess Senua: call three times, "Senua, Senua, Senua."

Swirl the water clockwise three times.

Make your pledge.

As the water stills you see the face of a woman looking at you. Is she young, or in middle age? Or is she older, perhaps ancient in years?

She smiles at you and there is such beauty in her smile, understanding and wisdom. She nods her head, accepting your pledge.

A light breeze blows across the still water and the woman's face is rippled and disappears.

Notice something glinting at the bottom of the pool. Reach down and pull out a beautiful circular silver and gold pendant on a chain.

What is the symbol on the front of the pendant?

On the back of the pendant are the words of your pledge. Read them to yourself or simply "know" them.

Place the pendant round your neck. Give thanks and bless the water of the spring and give thanks to Senua.

As you stand up you feel calm, peaceful, strong and energised. Walk back along the path by the hawthorn, then across the meadow. Enjoy the poppies, chamomile, buttercups and daisies.

You reach the country lane and see the three ash trees. As you walk between the ash trees find yourself in your safe place.

Sit in your safe place.

Breathe in peace, and release

Breathe in joy, and release

Breathe in love, and release

When you are ready open your eyes.

You are back. Welcome home.

The Three Mothers

Three times I come to you
And lay my harvest down.

To you, fair maid, I give my fruit,
Strawberries ripe, juicy, sweet,
Lick your fingers, tongue stained red; carefree youth.

To you, mother, I give my grain,
Golden wheat, barley, oats,
Make finest ale, and malted bread; a stomach full.

To you, grandmother, I give my dreams,
Hopes, fears, and those once known,
Hold me close, as night draws on; wisdom I seek.

Ritual to Increase Abundance in our Lives

The Three Mothers:
they who bring abundance and fulfil my earthly needs

The Mothers of Cirencester

PURPOSE

To draw abundance to my life.

AIM

To ask for abundance by writing the request three times on orange paper, and amplifying it by imbibing the request with the energy of orange flowers, crystals, and spicy warming oils. Dedicate it three times to The Three Mothers.

AFFIRMATION

I live a life of abundance and am provided with all that I need, and more besides.

TIME

Lughnasadh, 1st August.

THE GODDESS

The Three Mothers (or Deae Matres in Roman/Latin) are known from Romano-Celtic iconography from both Europe and Britain. A representation on an engraved stone plaque was found at Cirencester dating from 2AD or 3AD, and shows three women sitting side by side with short knee-length clothing, holding baskets of bread and fruit. All are cloaked, and two have headdresses, possibly suggesting marriage. The uniform, front facing, themed image is an amalgamation of the more abstract Celtic art forms with more personal, detailed Roman carving.

In Celtic art we repetitively find symbols and images carved three times over. The number three, and the repetition three times of an image, conveys the accumulation of the desired empowerment. Prior to the 1st Century AD, the Celts conveyed the concept of deity and spirituality in abstract terms using patterns and symbols. During the first to third centuries AD there was a merger between the Roman interest in the body and Celtic stylistic abstraction of decorative art forms. The resulting synthesis is shown in stone reliefs such as the Three Mothers, Coventina, Suliveae and the androgynous Genii Cuclatti.

In pagan imagery and symbolism, the concept of invoking spiritual energies three times over still exists. We consider the three leafed white clover and the Irish shamrock lucky. The rock carvings at Newgrange, north of Dublin, portray three wheeled spirals. The Isle of Man's flag is an ancient image of three legs. The neo-pagan movement has adopted the goddess in three guises: maiden, mother and crone. This is not only an ancient concept, but one that has developed over the millennia and is now recognised by the Neo-pagan and Wiccan movements. Today it is standard practice to cast a circle three times, repeat a chant three times, invoke the Goddess and God three times and ask for requests three times.

ABUNDANCE

What is evoked by the word abundance? For many the word, "abundance" provokes strong feelings and emotions. Abundance, for many people, is linked powerfully to what they do *not* have, and what they perceive somebody else to have. Emotions such as envy and jealousy are raised. The suggestion that living in abundance, with all that you need, want, and more besides, is wrong. So many people in the world do not live in material abundance and it can seem that to live in a state of overflowing abundance is not a good thing, but rather selfish, or that gains have been made at others' expense.

But, why do we wish poverty on ourselves? And are we impoverished, or is it a state of mind? Let's consider money. Money is a symbol. It symbolises the exchange of time and skill, and was created by humans for their convenience. Money has been used since pre-Roman times, with documented use being made of coins by the Iceni, Dubunni, Atrebates, Trinovantes, and Corieltauvi tribes. Hoards of coins have been unearthed in burial sites and in places where wealth was buried for safe keeping.

Throughout history, there has been a conflict between the amount of money a person is paid for work done, and the cost of goods, taxes paid, that comprise "The Cost of Living". Nowadays people do not want to work to survive, they want a rich and fulfilled leisure time as well. Money means travel, holidays, social events, and creative projects. It buys access to the environment where leisure activities take place, and buys the tuition needed to learn new skills. Whether it is a sport, or the desire to paint a picture, create a garden, travel to experience other cultures, or simply rest in the sun, money is needed.

Without money, a person is diminished. The artist cannot buy paint, the writer cannot buy the computer, the gardener cannot buy plants and equipment, and the traveller cannot fly abroad. But to earn enough money to do everything that is desired is difficult as the money is an exchange for time and skill, so jobs that earn the greater money usually take up more hours in the week, therefore stopping that person doing the very activity they are trying to earn enough money to implement. Life is a balancing act, and part of recognising "abundance" is being aware of what can be done with what one has, and ensuring that which is important is completed.

CORRESPONDENCES

CORNUCOPIA

The horn shaped basket overflowing with fruit and flowers has become symbolic of the fertile mother goddess, who provides an abundant harvest during the cycle of the year, and keeps people in plenty. This symbolism is found as early as 5 BC. Wicker baskets overflowing with bread, flowers and food are found portrayed on many carved reliefs of mother goddesses throughout Europe.

ORANGE

The colour orange supports change, and can be used to promote activity and opportunity. It is the colour of vitality, creativity and enthusiasm. The sacral chakra resonates to the colour orange and relates to creative fertility, sexuality and self-expression. It is located just below the naval in the abdominal region of the body. By using orange paper, ink, crystals, ribbons and flowers in the ritual we are bringing the vibration of orange to enhance our request.

MARIGOLDS

The Marigold (*Calendula officinalis*) is a hardy annual with bright orange petals. Its properties are antiseptic, soothing and healing. It can be used as the basis for healing ointments, salves and creams. Sow the seeds in March and after a quick germination they will flower throughout the summer months and into the early Autumn.

CRYSTALS

Tigers Eye is a golden brown crystal produced by limonite fibres embedded in quartz giving the stone a wonderful sheen. It strengthens resolve and courage, helps with decision making and promotes the correct use of power. It is said to stimulate the accumulation of wealth. It resonates with the Solar Plexus, Fire and Earth.

Amber is a tree resin that has mineralised over millions of years. It has been used for healing and protection for over 7000 years. It encourages self-confidence and happiness and promotes trusting self belief. Amber encourages creativity and the motivation needed to bring success. It resonates with the Solar Plexus and Fire.

Carnelian is a translucent orange stone and member of the Chalcedony group. It is a powerful motivator and helps with problem solving. It promotes courage and the willingness to keep going in times of difficulty. It promotes self-esteem and helps build confidence. It supports the driving force of ambition. It resonates with the Sacral Chakra and Fire.

Orange Calcite is a translucent orange stone formed from solutions containing carbon. It brings strength to overcome difficulties, promotes stability and helps personal development. Calcite can be used to encourage the transformation of concepts and ideas into actions that result in a positive outcome. It instigates success, energy and hard work. It resonates with the Sacral Chakra and Earth.

Red Jasper is an opaque red-brown stone of the quartz group containing iron oxide. It stimulates determination and the desire to achieve goals. Jasper promotes courage, will power, and helps bring ideas into actuality. It stimulates energy and dynamism. It resonates with the Base Chakra and Fire.

Garnet is a deep red crystal from the group called Island Silicates. It helps in very difficult situations that seem impossible, and encourages self survival, self confidence and strength of character. It promotes the dissolution of habits and thought patterns that get in the way of living in abundance. It resonates with the Base Chakra and Fire.

EQUIPMENT

The Altar:
   A symbol for the Goddess: a marigold plant
   Altar cloths in the colour of orange
   A sun symbol drawn on orange paper

The Elements:
   Air element: a censor or joss stick of warm spicy incense
   Fire element: an orange candle
   Water element: a chalice of spring water
   Earth element: a pentacle containing salt

Ritual Items:
   Orange paper
   An orange or red pen
   Orange wool or string
   Scissors
   An orange pouch or bag
   Abundance Blend of the following essential oils in sunflower
      seed oil: benzoin, ginger, neroli, cinnamon, sweet orange and
      bergamot
   A dish for the Essential Oil blend
   Orange and red crystals

Libation:

Ginger cake, or a fruit and honey bread, and wine, spiced cider or ale

The Four Directions:

East: yellow candle
South: red candle
West: blue candle
North: green candle

THE RITUAL

1. Set up the altar, and place the ritual items next to it.
2. Set the four candles at each of the four directions.
3. Cast the Circle.
4. Call in the Four Directions:

    Face the East: "I call in the Spirit of the Guardian of the East, of Air, the Sunrise, and the Spring. Hail and welcome." Light the yellow candle.

    Face the South: "I call in the Spirit of the Guardian of the South, of Fire, the Noon, and the Summer. Hail and welcome." Light the red candle.

    Face the West: "I call in the Spirit of the Guardian of the West, of Water, the Setting Sun, and the Autumn. Hail and welcome." Light the blue candle.

    Face the North: "I call in the Spirit of the Guardian of the North, of Earth, Midnight, and the Winter. Hail and welcome." Light the green candle.

5. Sprinkle a very little salt in the water. "I purify this water with the element of earth. I bring earth and water to this ritual. Blessed be."
6. Light the incense. "I bring the element of air to this ritual. Blessed be."
7. Light the orange candle. "I bring the element of fire to this ritual. Blessed be."

8. Call in the Three Mothers:

"I call in the Three Mothers, who bring us a full, rich harvest, abundance and pleasure to our lives, please be welcome in this circle. I ask your loving blessing on this ritual. May it be for the highest good of all. Hail and welcome!"

9. State the purpose of the ritual: "This ritual is to bring abundance to . . . . situation." (*Name the specific situation.*)

10. Raise energy by walking nine times round the circle chanting:

"Ladies of the Harvest,
Mother, Mother, Mother,
Come and celebrate,
With fruit and grain and wine."

Use drums, dance, whistles and pipes to celebrate the ritual.

Feel the energy build up, the expectation of a good result strengthen, and the power of the Goddesses become manifest.

11. Settle in front of the altar and pick up the orange paper, and the orange pen. Write your request on the paper, with your desire for bringing abundance to it.

Cut a marigold flower from the plant with thanksgiving, and dip it in the essential oil "Abundance Blend". Place the paper and the marigold inside the orange pouch and add crystals of your choice. Give thanks. Take the orange wool or string, cut a suitable length for wrapping nine times around your parcel. Wrap the wool or string around your parcel nine times and each time state:

"Three Mothers, I draw abundance to my request, and ask you to bless it for the highest good of all."

Finish with a knot and two long loose ends.

Dedicate the parcel through the elements and state the affirmation:

"I live a life of abundance and am provided with all that I need and more besides."

Place on the altar. It will be tied onto a tree branch at the end of the ritual.

12. Spend some time grounding yourself. Now is the time to eat the cake and drink the ale, reserving some for the Three Mothers. This can be placed outside after closing the circle.

13. Give thanks and say farewell to the Goddess:

"Three Mothers, Goddesses of Abundance and the over-flowing harvest, I thank you for being part of this ritual and bestowing your blessing on . . . . *(name the situation).* Go if you must, stay if you will. Hail and farewell." Blow out the orange candle.

14. Give thanks and say farewell to the Spirits of the Four Directions.

Move to the North: "Spirit of the Guardian of the North, of Earth, Midnight and Winter, thank you for being part of this ritual. Go if you must, stay if you will. Hail and farewell." Blow out the green candle.

Move to the West: "Spirit of the Guardian of the West, of Water, the Setting Sun and Autumn, thank you for being part of this ritual. Go if you must, stay if you will. Hail and farewell." Blow out the blue candle.

Move to the South: "Spirit of the Guardian of the South, of Fire, Noon, and Summer, thank you for being part of this ritual. Go if you must, stay if you will. Hail and farewell." Blow out the red candle.

Move to the East: "Spirit of the Guardian of the East, of Air, the Sunrise and Spring, thank you for being part of this ritual. Go if you must, stay if you will. Hail and farewell." Blow out the yellow candle.

15. Walk round the circle fluffing up the boundary and restoring the space to the physical realm.

16. Place the libation outside.

17. Hang the pouch up on a tree and leave it to do its work.

WHAT TO DO NEXT

Review your life and decide what your basic needs are and what you consider to be luxuries and enjoyable activities. Some parts of your lifestyle may be draining your resources, while others bring pleasure, enrichment and enjoyment. Strike a balance and take action on those aspects of your life that are unnecessary and wasteful. Contemplate your values and how they affect your life. What needs to change? What do you want to keep? Ask yourself if you are still enjoying products that you have been using as part of your lifestyle, or whether more economical versions of them will suffice allowing the release of cash for other ventures. Come to terms with the fact that abundance is not only about money. Some of the most valuable experiences come free. Make a list of abundance in your life that has no price.

MEDITATION

Close your eyes and relax. Breathe deeply in, allowing the air to be drawn right down to your belly. Then let it go very slowly and gently. Repeat this twice more.

Create a protective bubble of white light around yourself. This is a secure place to which you can return at any time. Hold the image in your mind. You are sitting in the very centre, surrounded by white light. This will not let anything harm you. You are protected and safe.

Your safe place shapes itself into a meadow of wild flowers. A path leads down the centre of the meadow. At either side of the pathway are wide borders of chamomile flowers and poppies. Walk along the path. The sun is warm, but a soft, gentle breeze cools you. Follow the path to an orchard, and here you find a small green gate that opens into the orchard. Go inside. Here you encounter plum trees laden with ripe plums, golden pink Victorias, Greengages and dark purple Damsons. You see pear trees, apple trees and ripe sweet cherry trees. Pluck a cherry from the nearest tree and taste it, letting the pip fall to the floor.

A woman is looking at you from behind the tree. She is of middle age, with a wise, kind face and green robes edged with crimson. She smiles and asks you, "What do you need?" You answer honestly. Tell her what you would like to change about your life. Tell her where you feel impoverished. She pulls a golden pear off a tree and says, "Eat this." Take a bite of the sweet, juicy pear and feel its golden strength surging inside you. You feel satisfied and full, and can see how you can positively change the situation so that you are not impoverished. Reflect on this as you eat the rest of the pear.

Thank the woman and she moves away from you, gliding between the trees into the depths of the orchard.

Walk on through the orchard and through a small rustic gate into a field of golden wheat. It is ripe and ready for harvest. Pluck an ear of wheat and rub the grain between your fingers. Chew on a grain of wheat letting the husk fall to the ground.

A second woman emerges from the cornfield. Maybe she has been there all the time. She too, is of middle age, kindly and wise in appearance, wearing a green robes edged with gold. She looks at you smiling and asks, "What do you need?" You answer honestly. You may state the same need as before, over again. Or maybe you have another need. Ask the woman for help.

She pulls three ears of wheat and fashions them into a corn dolly. She gives them to you and says, "Keep this with you." As you hold the corn dolly you feel the golden strength of the corn running up your arms and into your heart, then down into your solar plexus. You feel stronger, satisfied, and excited. You can see clearly how to improve your situation.

Thank the woman and she walks into the wheat and seems to become one with it, disappearing from your view.

Follow a narrow path between the wheat and a hawthorn hedge, laden with haw berries. You come to a grey stone building with a blue, wooden door in it. Push the door and walk inside, glad to be in the cool of the simple building. See a smooth stone flagged floor, and notice dark oak beams in the ceiling. There is a plain window letting in sunlight, situated high up in the wall. At the back of the building is a small wooden table with a golden goblet on it, filled with liquid. Pick up the goblet and look at it. It is beautifully engraved with fruit and flowers.

You hear footsteps behind you, and turn to face a third woman. She is wearing green robes edged with white. Like the first two women, she is of middle age with a wise and kind face. She asks, "What do you need?" Tell her honestly. You may need more advice on your first need, or you may have a third need to divulge. She says, "Drink from the cup." Drink the golden liquid. It has a familiar taste yet fills you with tingling, sparkling energy. You feel energised and strong and are able to take on your challenges. You understand that these challenges are ensuring you develop and grow in wisdom and strength. Stop fighting your problems, needs and desires and instead know you will find solutions.

You thank the woman, and she seems to fade into a patch of sunlight filtering hazily through the window on the wall.

Replace the goblet on the table, and turn to face the door. Walk through the door and find yourself in your safe place.

Sit in your safe place.

Breathe in peace, and release

Breathe in joy, and release

Breathe in love, and release

When you are ready, open your eyes.

You are back. Welcome home.

Coventina

It's a cold northern wind that blasts across the moors,
Blowing water from my bowl,
Tossing around carelessly,
Water I've collected,
Year upon year.

Light shatters against the falling drops,
Breaking them into fragments,
Scattering purples, greens and reds,
I have to ask, "Where is the gold?"

I tread on orange and yellow,
When the autumnal leaves drop quietly,
Decorating pavements,
Heaping against walls.

I catch azure and indigo,
Between dark clouds,
When that strong northern air forces them apart,
Revealing fisherman's blue.

The gold I found was fools' gold,
I threw it down on the beach and turned to depart,
A thousand pieces glittered on the sand,
While a gull screamed a solitary song.

I tip my bowl over,
Watch streams cascade and foam around my feet,
Rivulets find their own way down,
Down, to the pool of Coventina.
It's a cold northern wind.

Ritual to Bring Healing

Coventina: she who dwells by the sacred well

Goddess of the Sacred Spring at Brocolitia, Northumberland

PURPOSE

To bring physical healing to the body.

AIM

To make a medicine bundle representing healing power, and dedicate it to Coventina, to invoke healing within one's body.

A small amount of preparation is needed in advance. Make a figurine from air-dry clay or salt dough depicting yourself and portraying any physical ailment. Inscribe your name on it. After making this, you may want to paint it or dress it. The figurine should be made one or two weeks in advance.

AFFIRMATION

My body is whole and well.

TIME

Autumn Equinox, September.

THE GODDESS

Coventina's presence in the north of England is evidenced by more than by ten inscriptions found at a sacred temple dedicated to Coventina, near the Roman Camp of Carrawburgh, on Hadrian's Wall in Northumberland. Coventina's temple, along with a temple to the Roman God Mithras, and another temple to three nymphs, were located at the Fort of Brocolitia (Badger Holes). The temple was built at the source of the natural spring that still bubbles forth today, known as Meggie's Dene Burn. Such springs were revered by the Brythons, as a fresh water source was the key to living a healthy life.

The temple for Coventina was excavated in 1876 by John Clayton, who had previously discovered the Roman Bath House in 1873. In 1849 the Temple of Mithras was unearthed, and in 1859 a Temple to three water nymphs was revealed. Given the terrain, the spring, the pure water and the Brythonic traditions, it would be reasonable to expect that the local population would have been worshipping Coventina long before the Romans took up residence. It is likely that the practice was adopted by the Roman cohorts who inhabited the fort, used the adjacent baths, and worshipped in the temple of Mithras.

Altogether over ten inscriptions have been found etched onto altar stones and pottery incense burners during the excavation of the fort. The inscriptions show that the Romans invoked Coventina for general blessings and petitions. Coins, jewellery and gifts were thrown into the water, and statuettes and votive offerings represented the person who was making the petition or asking for healing. Money is symbolic of one's life energy, and was given in exchange for blessings. In effect, by giving coins, a person is giving part of their life. The coins found are dated AD407. Other objects, such as figurines show a clear example of how sympathetic magic was invoked by the Brythons and the Romans. Someone with a painful leg might dedicate a statuette with a bound leg to Coventina and ask for healing as they laid in Coventina's well.

There are no myths and stories surrounding Coventina. Simply the archaeological remains of a society that invoked a water nymph, and asked her help in healing, birth, death, oaths, petitions, and requests, and who was significant enough for the Roman invaders to adopt her.

These days, Coventina's Well can still be visited, and the sacred spring flows in a boggy area next to the stone walls of the Temple of Mithras.

SUBJECT: HEALING

When a person feels unwell, becomes ill or their body ceases to function in a balanced and healthy manner, physical healing is the primary concern. It is in our physical body that we first notice the pain, functions that become difficult, or we experience sensations we do not understand and that are not comfortable. When we feel pain, we seek help.

Holistic healing treats the whole body, and this includes the electrical energy field that surrounds the body, known as the aura. When the aura is out of balance or diminished, physical illness can follow. The aura is complex, but most holistic therapists and healers agree that it is the place of the emotional, mental and spiritual bodies as well as the physical body.

A person who is unforgiving and retains within themselves a great amount of anger will suffer emotionally and mentally. This may result in stomach ulcers, headaches, a lowering of the immune system that allows all manner of coughs, colds, influenza, stomach complaints and other viruses to get through and cause the physical body to become unwell.

145

People who are stressed may experience a low immune system, tiredness, fatigue, depression, anxiety, become clumsy and start to have accidents more frequently.

When we consider that emotions are heavily affected by hormones, and that hormones are chemicals, chemicals are physical, yet the outcome is a state of mind, we can see how closely entwined the physical, emotional, mental and spiritual bodies are.

Someone who enjoys a spiritual walk, yet who is thwarted in this by family, job, housing or friends may also experience a negative physical, emotional and mental outcome.

The ritual to bring about healing is not only for the physical body. Analyse your need for healing, and if it is a physical symptom, ask for guidance to see if it is rooted in another cause that needs healing first: the emotional body, the mental body or the spiritual body.

CORRESPONDENCES

POURING WATER

The Goddess Coventina is depicted in triplicity on an engraving in a stone bas relief found at the Temple of Coventina at Carrawburgh. The Three Water Nymphs that were found in Coventina's well depict three women draped in robes, holding one water pot in an uplifted hand, and a second pot pouring water in a lower hand. Each woman sits separately in her own archway separated by pillars, asymetrically typical of the carvings of the Celtic tradition. The image anticipates the picture on the tarot card, "The Star," in which the single figure of a female pours water from a vessel in each hand, and also, "Temperance," an angel that pours water from one vessel to the other, one water pot held in each hand. Such concepts are universal and found depicted in symbolic imagery throughout history. The feminine connection with water, holding of water within a vessel, and pouring forth the water from the vessel, all signify the same root of fertility, balance, and the sanctity of life.

MEDICINE BUNDLES

Medicine bundles originate from the Native American Indian tradition, and similar bundles and bags were kept by Shamans in Scandinavian countries. Native American Indian medicine bundles have been handed down from generation to generation. They held seeds, nuts, pine cones, horsehair, skins, arrowheads, rocks and grasses. Once made, they were wrapped and secured and never allowed to touch the ground. The bundles were considered holy and sacred and their purpose was to aid ritual.

The purpose of the medicine bundle is to gather together and focus the energy of significant items, corresponding to, and symbolising the physical healing needs of a person. In our ritual we will make a medicine bundle and dedicate it to Coventina in a similar manner to our Roman and Brythonic forebears, who dedicated statuettes, personal items and coins to her. The focal point of the bundle will be a figurine, male or female (depending on whether you, the petitioner, are male of female) with whatever part of the body that needs healing bound three times over. The figurine is a proxy for oneself.

THREE LEAFED PLANTS

The three leafed plants native to Britain tend to be members of the legume family Fabaceae, under the genus Trifolium. This includes the "lucky" white clovers, Ireland's shamrock, and other flowers such as black medick. These are considered lucky because of their tri-part leaves that are symbolic of the tri-part Goddess.

Use clover flowers and leaves during the ritual to float on Coventina's water bowl and place them as an offering within the medicine bundle.

Red clover flowers make an excellent balancing infusion for women to drink, as the plant releases plant-oestrogens that support the body during times of premenstrual tension and the menopause.

SACRED WELLS

Sacred wells and water sources still fascinate, and modern evidence of superstition and belief can be seen at a surprisingly huge amount of wells, springs, tanks and even the most tenuous of drainage channels as people make their wishes and cast a coin in the water, hoping that "someone" or "something" grants their request. Fountains in shopping centres are often a focal point for the shopping fraternity and though obviously man-made, fulfil some need in humans to exchange hard earned cash for prayer requests, by throwing coins in the water.

In The White Peak District of Derbyshire, the abode of Arnemetia, well dressing festivals can be enjoyed in the summer months between May and September as local villages, clubs, guilds and societies create beautiful backdrops to over fifty different wells from natural materials such as flower petals, seeds, berries, herbs, leaves and moss. A paper design is overlaid on a wet clay covered wooden board, and the outline of the design pricked through into the clay. After removing the design overlay the decorative materials are pressed into the clay. The finished board is situated next to or behind the well, displaying the image which is usually from the Bible or depicting locally relevant or national events. The well sometimes is designated a "Well Queen" and blessing ceremonies are held, mixing Christianity with ancient reminiscences of fertility rites.

Over time, many wells became associated with Saints such as St Leven's Well in Cornwall and St Winifred's Well in Flintshire. Many also had their own specialism, such as the well of St Kilda's Isle, believed to heal deafness and disorders of the mind. The Christian Church, if it could not eliminate rustic pagan beliefs, could transform them into a Christianised version acceptable to all. The well was approached with reverence, and with sacrificial gifts to the Genius Loci. Pins and needles, coins and rags of material were all acceptable. The rags were tied to nearby bushes and trees while the petitioner made their request. Rag trees are common in countries such as Cyprus, and for those with a sharp eye, evidence exists that the practice continues in Britain today.

COLOUR HEALING

Bear these colours in mind when choosing coloured materials, wool and ribbons for your medicine bundle.

Brown—earth, grounding, order, conventionalism, practicality, materialism, concentration

Red—energy, action, passion, strength, confidence, courage, vitality, aggression, temper

Pink—love, self-love, unconditional love, beauty

Orange—creativity, vitality, enthusiasm

Yellow—joy, happiness, intellect, clarity of thought, stimulation

Gold—wealth, prosperity, understanding

Green—balance, harmony, calming, refreshing, prosperity, fertility

Blue—communication, cooling, emotional calm, inspiration, tranquillity, peace

Indigo—mental powers, calming, psychic powers, relaxation, reassurance

Purple—spirituality, power, royalty, sensuality, enlightenment, wealth, wisdom

White—purity, cleansing, truth, protection, innocence

Black—absence of colour, mystery, the unconscious, absorption, authority, power.

The Earth Chakra: brown

The Base Chakra: red

The Sacral Chakra: orange

The Solar Plexus: yellow

The Heart Chakra: green

The Chakra between the Heart and the Throat: turquoise

The Throat Chakra: blue

The Brow Chakra: indigo

The Crown Chakra: violet

The Soul Star Chakra (above the head): white

FEMININE PLANTS

African Violet, Apple, Apricot, Avocado, Lemon Balm, Barley, Bedstraw, Beech, Birch, Blackberry, Cherry, Coltsfoot, Columbine, Comfrey, Cowslip, Cyclamen, Cypress, Daffodil, Daisy, Elder, Elm, Feverfew, Foxglove, Geranium, Heather, Honesty, Hyacinth, Iris, Ivy, Ladies Mantle, Lilac, Orchid, Pansy, Plum, Poppy, Primrose, Raspberry, Rose, Spearmint, Strawberry, Sweet Pea, Thyme, Tulip, Vervain, Valerian, Violet, Yarrow, Yew.

MASCULINE PLANTS

Alder, Almond, Ash, Aspen, Basil, Bay, Bistort, Borage, Bracken, Broom, Carnations, Cedar, Celandines, Chamomile, Chrysanthemums, Coriander, Dandelion, Dill, Dock, Endives, Fennel, Ferns, Garlic, Gorse, Hawthorn, Hazel, Holly, Honeysuckle, Horse Chestnut, Juniper, Larch, Lavender, Lemon Verbena, Linden, Liverwort, Lovage, Maple, Marigold, Marjoram, Mint, Mistletoe, Nettle, Oak, Parsley, Pennyroyal, Peony, Pine, Reeds, Lily, Magnolia, Mugwort, Mullein, Rosemary, Rowan, Sage, Snapdragon, Sunflowers, Thistle, Toadflax.

EQUIPMENT

The Altar:
    Symbol for the Goddess: spring water in a bowl and a bunch of
        clover flowers and leaves
    Altar cloths in blues, greens, silvers

The Elements:
    Air, Fire and Water: essential oils in an essential oil diffuser
    Earth : rock salt on a dish

Ritual Items:
    A figurine made in advance from air-dry clay or salt dough

Three bindings: coloured ribbon or wool
A doily
Coloured cloth
Ribbon or wool to tie a wrapping on the figurine
Flower, herbs, leaves, nuts, seeds, crystals
Paper ticket and a pen
Essential oils
Matches

Libation:
Cakes and Ale

The Four Directions:
East: yellow candle
South: red candle
West: blue candle
North: green candle

THE RITUAL

1. Set up the altar, and place the ritual items next to it.
2. Set the four coloured candles at each of the four directions.
3. Cast the Circle.
4. Call in the Four Directions:
   Face the East:
   "I call in the Spirit of the Guardian of the East, of Air, the Sunrise, and the Spring. Hail and welcome." Light the yellow candle.
   Face the South:
   "I call in the Spirit of the Guardian of the South, of Fire, the Noon, and the Summer. Hail and welcome." Light the red candle.
   Face the West:

"I call in the Spirit of the Guardian of the West, of Water, the Setting Sun, and the Autumn. Hail and welcome." Light the blue candle.

Face the North:

"I call in the Spirit of the Guardian of the North, of Earth, Midnight, and the Winter. Hail and welcome." Light the green candle.

5. Place essential oils on the water on the essential oil diffuser. Light the candle. "I bring the elements of air, fire and water to this ritual. Blessed be."

6. Hold up the dish of rock salt. "I bring earth to this ritual. Blessed be."

8. Call in the Goddess:

"I call in the Goddess Coventina of the sacred spring at Brocolitia, please be welcome in this circle. May it be for the highest good of all. Hail and welcome!" Float some clover flowers and leaves on the bowl of water.

9. State the purpose of the ritual: "This ritual is to bring physical healing to my body".

(Be specific as to what part, the condition and the healing needed.)

10. Raise energy by walking nine times round the circle chanting:

"Coventina, Coventina, Coventina,
Sacred Goddess of the Water, of the Water, of the Water,
Bring me healing, bring me healing, bring me healing,
I welcome you into my circle now.

Pick up the bowl from the altar with both hands and hold it high.

Feel the energy of the Goddess, draw it to yourself, contain it, hold it, and give thanks.

Replace the bowl on the altar.

152

11. Settle down by the altar and take a piece of cloth. Lay it out. Then place the doily on top. This is the outer wrapping of your medicine bundle.

    Write your request for healing on a piece of paper and tie it to the figurine's relevant body part. Bind the same part of the body three times, using a separate piece of ribbon or wool each time. State your request for healing three times over as you bind the body part three times.

    Lay the figurine on the doily. Now add herbs, flowers, foliage, nuts, seeds, crystals, and sprinkle with essential oils. Wrap the material round the bundle, so the contents do not fall out, and tie with a ribbon or wool.

    Dedicate the bundle through air, fire, water and earth as you dedicate it to Coventina and ask her blessing and healing. Lay the bundle on the altar.

12. State the affirmation, "My body is whole and well." Give thanks.

13. Spend some time grounding yourself. Now is the time to eat the cakes and ale, reserving some for Coventina. This can be laid outside after closing the circle.

14. Give thanks and say farewell to the Goddess:

    "Thank you Coventina for your healing. I look forward to experiencing it within my body. Go if you must, stay if you will. Hail and farewell."

15. Give thanks and say farewell to the Guardian Spirits of the Four Directions.

    Move to the North:

    "Spirit of the Guardian of the North, of Earth, of Midnight, and of Winter, thank you for being in this circle and part of this ritual. Go if you must, stay if you will, hail and farewell." Put out the green candle.

    Move to the West:

    "Spirit of the Guardian of the West, of Water, the Setting Sun, and the Autumn, thank you for being in this circle and part of this ritual. Go if you must, stay if you will, hail and farewell." Put out the blue candle.

Move to the South:

"Spirit of the Guardian of the South, of Fire, the Noon, and the Summer, thank you for being in this circle and part of this ritual. Go if you must, stay if you will, hail and farewell." Put out the red candle.

Move to the East:

"Spirit of the Guardian of the East, of Air, the Sunrise, and the Spring, thank you for being in this circle and part of this ritual. Go if you must, stay if you will, hail and farewell." Put out the yellow candle.

16. Walk round the circle fluffing up the boundary and restoring the space to the physical realm.

17. Place the libation outside.

WHAT HAPPENS NEXT

Look after yourself. Never give up taking medication without the doctor's permission. Expect and look forward to healing. It does not often happen in a split second, but may take time. Watch out for intuitive promptings to change your lifestyle and try to accommodate these. Sometimes healing is a result of change of habit. The Goddess will support you in this. Eat wholesome food and drink plenty of water. Rest enough, and give yourself some time out. Fresh air and exercise is usually highly beneficial. Communicating with the Goddess often means that you are encouraged to align yourself with healthy practices rather than following unhealthy ways.

MEDITATION

Close your eyes and relax. Breathe deeply in, allowing the air to be drawn right down to your belly. Then let it go very slowly and gently. Repeat this twice more.

Create a protective bubble of white light around yourself. This is a secure place to which you can return at any time. Hold the image in your mind. You are sitting in the very centre surrounded by a sphere of light. This will not let anything harm you. You are protected and safe.

Your safe place shapes itself into a grassy mound on which sheep graze contentedly. Once a Roman Fort was built here, but now there is nothing left but the shape of the mound and some rocks. Walk over the grassy mound, and take a broad path that leads you over a small tumbling stream running downhill into a small, still pool, surrounded with grass, plants and moss.

Sit by the pool on a flat rock by the water. Notice the wild flowers and grasses that surround the pool. You see red and white clover, marsh marigolds, and chamomile. The breeze ripples the surface of the water. As the water becomes still again, you see your reflection in the water. Bring your attention to the part of your body that needs healing.

You hear someone approach. As you look behind you, you see a tall woman carrying an empty water jug. She seems to move with the sunbeams, caught in a rainbow of light.

Coventina looks at you, and you tell her which part of you needs healing.

Coventina dips her water jug in the pool and pours the water over your body. It is cold, yet sparkles with healing energy. She fills the jug and pours water over your body again. You feel strong and balanced. She fills the jug and pours water over your body for the third time. You are filled with joy. You feel the energy of the water healing you.

She plucks a red clover from the side of the pool and gives it to you. Hold it, look at the three leaves; three leaves for the Goddess three times invoked. When you look up Coventina is fading into a rainbow of water and light. Look into the pool and see your own reflection once more.

In your pocket there is a silver coin. Throw a coin into the pool and give thanks to Coventina.

Spend time resting by the side of the pool. When you are ready, stand and follow the path back over the stream, to the mound of grass and rocks. A wooden gate leads back to the road. As you walk through the wooden gate you find yourself back in your safe place.

Sit in your safe place.

Breathe in peace, and release

Breathe in joy, and release

Breathe in love, and release

When you are ready, open your eyes.

You are back. Welcome home.

Ratis

I stand on the hilltop and I watch,
Watch for a sign in the stars,
Listen for the sound of change in the wind.
The beacon is lit,
Fire dances, embracing the air,
Warning, warning,
They come.

Stealthy at midnight,
When the moon hides her face,
Clouds cover the sky,
And the stars move within.

Yet the fire burns bright.
Read the fire, the fire of warning,
I feel you on the wind,
I feel your breath on my cheek,
I hear your whisper, so soft, so close.

Raise the alarm,
We defend,
Integrity, honesty, sacrifice,
We are not yours to plunder,
Fight to the death.

I die in honour and truth,
Beside the beacon,
It lights my way
Through shadow and silhouette
To the dark lands,
Stillness, I am.

Where will you go?
What have you found,
That makes plunder worthwhile?
I am rich within, but out of time,
And take with me,
All that I am.

Ritual for Protection

Ratis: she who provides a fortress to protect me

Goddess of the hill forts of Northumberland

PURPOSE

To protect myself from my own actions, other people's actions and words, and situations that destroy me.

AIM

Make an amulet using seasonal protective tree branches, leaves, fruit and a crystal.

AFFIRMATION

I am protected within and protected without.

TIME

Samhain, 31st October.

THE GODDESS

Ratis is the Goddess of the Iron Age hill forts of Northumberland. A Roman altar, inscribed with her name, has been found at Birdoswald and can be viewed in Chesters Museum. She may have been a Goddess local to the area around Hadrian's Wall, as no further inscriptions have been discovered in other areas of Britain.

As with many Iron Age Goddesses, the evidence has been documented by the invading Romans who Latinized the Brythonic name of the Goddess. It is possible that the Romans personified the concept of the Goddess of the protective hill fort. Hill forts were indigenous to the Celtic communities. For the purpose of this ritual we invoke Ratis as the Goddess of Protection, who builds a fortress round us in our times of need.

SUBJECT: PROTECTION

Iron Age hill forts were built on high ground so that good use could be made of the panorama, enabling the forewarning of enemy attack, and giving time to action defence and counter attack. It is much more difficult to successfully attack a structure placed on the top of a hill or mound. As we invoke the protection of Ratis, we ask her to place us on "the high ground" so that we can see situations as they really are, be forewarned about personal attack, and also be aware of what is happening around us so we don't make unnecessary mistakes.

Part of our protection is being aware of who we are, who we are with, the circumstances we are in and where this combination is leading. We say, "I didn't see this coming!" Without being overly paranoid, a certain watchfulness and vigilance is needed, and clarity of vision is necessary.

Often we leave ourselves open to attack, and people around us become aware of this and use our vulnerability to their advantage. Build a defence against bullying, harassment, emotional and physical abuse by making a change in lifestyle and attitude. Our defence needs to be built on a solid foundation. Sometimes we invite trouble which leaves a gaping hole in our defences. Whether it is carelessness, laziness, tiredness, a don't-care attitude or spending time in an unhelpful environment, our defences are weakened and we are left without protection. Major changes need to be actioned. It is not helpful simply to paper over the hole and hope all will be well.

If we allow small cracks to appear in our armour and then ignore them, we experience leakage of our energy and loss of strength. The consequences are weakness, irritability, exhaustion and the loss of "self". Analyse the cause of the leak and endeavour to stop it. This will enable you to regain your sense of "self" and become stronger, and you will become protected internally as well as externally.

CORRESPONDENCES

HEDGES

Thorn hedges are still used for protection, and are doubly useful because they provide pretty flowers and nourishing fruit during the year. Homesteads and cultivation were found within the hedge boundaries whilst the wild and dangerous forests stayed outside. The wise woman or man breached the hedge boundaries to hunt for medicinal herbs, hence the origin of the term "Hedge Witch".

The Wild Rose is admired for its beautiful flowers, and the rosehips are packed with Vitamin C. However, beware the rose's thorns. Sharp thorns bring protection to the homestead, whilst the rosehips bring protection to the body.

Hawthorn is a hard wood that, when burned, releases an extremely high heat. Its thorns are protective, and it grows profusely in the British climate. Hawthorn is used to create talismans and magical sachets to bring protection to the wearer.

Blackberry has fast growing runners and sharp thorns. However, it also carries beautiful flowers and nourishing fruit. A blackberry hedge will keep intruders out, but will also feed a family on its luscious fruit.

Rowan tree grows in high, inaccessible places on moorland, yet also survives city life in the modern age. City councils have realised that the hardy rowan will grow on street corners, and between dual carriageway lanes. The Rowan forms a tiny pentagram opposite its stalk declaring its protective nature, even though it has no thorns. Protective amulets were created by tying rowan twigs together in the shape of a cross. Often they have been carried for protection and sewn into battle clothing to protect the warrior.

AMULETS

Amulets are created specifically to protect the maker from trouble.

ESSENTIAL OILS

Black Pepper: Mars, Fire, Masculine energy, protection and courage.
Juniper: Sun, Fire, Masculine energy, banishes negative energy.

TOURMALINE

Tourmaline is the stone of Capricorn, the Earth and the base chakra. It brings protection, repels harmful energy, and brings clear thinking. Use Tourmaline for stress relief and for emotional and mental protection.

RED

Red is the colour that corresponds to the concepts of survival, fighting and defending, and fleeing to save oneself.

BINDING

Binding is symbolic, representing the binding of negative powers so they cannot harm.

EQUIPMENT

The Altar:
> Symbol for the Goddess: a branch of rose with rosehips (decorate it if you would like to)
> Altar cloths in earth colours of brown, rust, and green

The Elements:
> Air: essential oil diffuser and essential oils of black pepper and juniper
> Fire: red candle
> Water: a dish of natural spring water
> Earth: a dish of soil and pebbles

Ritual Items:
> Short branches, twigs and leaves of rowan, hawthorn, blackberry, and wild rose for making an amulet
> Red ribbons
> Red wool
> Scissors
> Tourmaline crystal
> Essential oils of black pepper and juniper
> Sunflower seed oil
> A small dish for the essential oil blend
> Matches

Libation:
> Blackberry cake and rosehip cordial

The Four Directions: a bundle of twigs, leaves and fruit tied with red ribbon

East: Wild Rose
South: Hawthorn
West: Blackberry
North: Rowan

THE RITUAL

1. Set up the altar, and place the ritual items next to it.
2. Set the four bundles of twigs and fruit at each of the four directions.
3. Cast the Circle.
4. Call in the Four Directions:

    Face the East: "I call in the Spirit of the Wild Rose. Hail and welcome."

    Face the South: "I call in the Spirit of the Hawthorn. Hail and welcome."

    Face the West: "I call in the Spirit of the Blackberry. Hail and welcome."

    Face the North: "I call in the Spirit of the Rowan. Hail and welcome."

5. Sprinkle a very little soil in the water. "I bring earth and water to this ritual. Blessed be."
6. Light the incense. "I bring the element of air to this ritual. Blessed be."
7. Light the red candle. "I bring the element of fire to this ritual. Blessed be."
8. Call in the Goddess Ratis:

    "I call in the Goddess Ratis, Lady of the hill forts, who brings protection within and without, please be welcome in this circle. I ask your loving blessing on this ritual. May it be for the highest good of all. Hail and welcome!"

9. State the purpose of the ritual: "This ritual is to bring protection for myself from my own actions, other peoples' actions and words, and situations that destroy me.

10. Raise energy by walking nine times round the circle chanting:

"Ratis, Ratis, Ratis,
Build your fortress round me,
Protector and defender,
Encircle me with your strength."

Feel the energy build up, the expectation of a good result strengthen, and the power of the Goddess become manifest.

11. Settle in front of the altar and pick up the twigs of rose, hawthorn, blackberry and rowan. Be careful not to prick your fingers. Make a small bundle of the twigs and fruits and bind in the tourmaline crystal. Wrap it around nine times with the red wool. You may want to make an even-armed cross, shape a person (yourself), or create a woven pattern. As you make your amulet, meditate on Ratis, your need for protection in your circumstances and situation, fortresses and clear vision. Focus specifically on any particular problem you need protection from. Hold your amulet between your hands and fill it with the energy of protection.

Take the finished amulet to Ratis, dedicate it through the elements. Mix black pepper and juniper essential oils with sunflower seed oil in a dish. Dip the amulet in the essential oil blend to seal the amulet's power. State the affirmation, "I am protected within and protected without."

12. Spend some time grounding yourself. Now is the time to eat the cake and drink the ale, reserving some for Ratis. This can be placed outside after closing the circle.

13. Give thanks and say farewell to the Goddess:

"Lady Ratis, Goddess of the hill fort, I thank you for being part of this ritual and bestowing your protection. Go if you must, stay if you will. Hail and farewell." Put out the red candle.

14. Give thanks and say farewell to the Spirits of the four trees.

Move to the North: "Spirit of the Rowan, thank you for being part of this ritual and protecting me. Go if you must, stay if you will. Hail and farewell."

Move to the West: "Spirit of the Blackberry, thank you for being part of this ritual and protecting me. Go if you must, stay if you will. Hail and farewell."

Move to the South: "Spirit of the Hawthorn, thank you for being part of this ritual and protecting me. Go if you must, stay if you will. Hail and farewell."

Move to the East: "Spirit of the Wild Rose, thank you for being part of this ritual and protecting me. Go if you must, stay if you will. Hail and farewell."

15. Walk round the circle fluffing up the boundary and restoring the space to the physical realm.

16. Place the libation outside.

17. Keep the amulet with you as you go about your daily life. If it is to protect your home, then place it near your front door.

WHAT TO DO NEXT

Without being over-obsessive, be vigilant and aware of what is going on. Don't leave yourself open to criticism, or seek out irresponsible company. When something does go wrong, then you will know that you have done your best. Notice when protection seems strongest and learn from those "near misses". Don't take Ratis' protection for granted, but work with the Goddess to keep her protection in place.

MEDITATION

Close your eyes and relax. Breathe deeply in, allowing the air to be drawn right down to your belly. Then let it go very slowly and gently. Repeat this twice more.

Create a protective bubble of white light around yourself. This is a secure place to which you can return at any time. Hold the image in your mind. You are sitting in the very centre, surrounded by white light. This will not let anything harm you. You are protected and safe.

Your safe place shapes itself into your home. Leave your home through the front door, and walk down a pathway next to a busy road. See a rowan tree growing on a patch of grass by the road. It grows, sturdy and straight, and is covered in green leaves and clusters of little red berries.

There is a green gate and a broad track leading to some fields. Walk through the gate, closing it behind you. The noise of traffic stops and peace descends. Follow the wide pathway between fields hedged with hawthorn. Notice the sharp protective thorns and understand why hawthorn is chosen by farmers to protect their fields.

You come to a patch of blackberries. The fruits are juicy and ripe. Pick some and eat them, being careful not to prick your fingers.

The path begins to climb upwards through some woodland. Enter the woods, and see sunlight filtering down through the branches of the trees, casting shadows on the mossy track. The path continues to slope upwards and you walk out of the woodland into a grassy area.

Looking upwards you see a steep grassy mound. It is terraced with ridges and you can see areas of rough hewn stones. The ridges encircle the hill. This was an ancient hill fort, although all that is left now is the mound on which it stood.

Climb the hill, spiralling up to the top using the ridges and terraces as a path. Look over the valley and see the town nestling below. Think of the people in the town . . . think of your friends . . . your family . . . colleagues at work . . . people in shops, offices, workplaces . . . all the people you come across during your daily life.

Some people are loving, generous and kind, but others are rude, arrogant, or lazy. Sometimes they blame other people for their own shortcomings. Do you do that as well? If you are angry with others, is it because you are also angry with yourself?

Do you want to live with an open and generous heart?

How can you protect yourself from people who would take advantage of that?

Do your circumstances and situations deliver justice?

Does injustice make you upset and angry, anxious and worried?

Do you care about what other people think?

Are you vigilant, journeying through your life with integrity?

Do you leave yourself wide open to criticism?

Spend some time pondering on your own behaviour.

Wisdom is gained through experience. Experience is sometimes hard, uncomfortable and difficult. It can make us unhappy and stressed.

Call Ratis' name three times:

"Ratis, Ratis, Ratis."

Ratis comes on the wind, blowing strongly from the North. As she comes, the wind blows around your body. It is cool and strong and the gusts of wind cleanse you of stress, anxiety, unhappiness, bitterness and anger. You feel at one with the gusting wind. Let the wind whisk away your negative emotions and freshen you.

Ratis, borne on the wind, whirls around you one more time, then suddenly she is gone. The wind dies down and a playful breeze caresses you. You are at peace.

You walk down the hill, through the woodland and as you approach the fields, you see a single pink rose blooming on a thorn bush. All around the rosehips are forming and you know you can pluck this last rose.

You walk back to town, carrying the rose and thanking Ratis for her protection.

When you see a front door you recognise as your own, you enter and find yourself in your safe place.

Sit in your safe place.

Breathe in peace, and release
Breathe in joy, and release
Breathe in love, and release
When you are ready, open your eyes.
You are back. Welcome home.

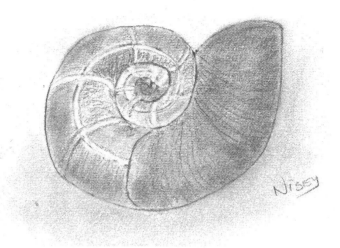

Cailleach

Follow the spiral of the Milky Way
Cascading diamonds turn inwards
Sliding, into the void.
Follow the whirlpool round, and around,
The powerful pull, dragging round and down,
Into the void.

Grandmother, reach into the centre,
Touch the darkness,
Where black chaos reigns,
And retrieve your wisdom.

Release the wind,
Wild white horses rage,
The Sea Gods rise in anger,
The wheel turns, and winter strikes.

Vicious claws tear hair and skin,
Freezing breath,
Whips red roses vivid on pallid cheeks,
Cloaks of wool spiral around.

Are you stone?
Rise from the snow and ice,
Give birth to the Spring,
Undo your cloak,
Reveal the Maiden within,
Turn the wheel again.

Ritual to Relinquish Guilt and Restore Integrity

Cailleach: she who washes her cloak clean in the whirlpool sea

Goddess of the Corryvreckan Whirlpool, Scotland

PURPOSE

To leave behind guilt, confess wrong doing, and restore integrity.

AIM

To walk into a spiral meditating on what issues are causing shame and guilt, release the shame and guilt, receive forgiveness and walk out of the spiral free.

AFFIRMATION

I am free of shame, and restored to full integrity.

TIME

November, the onset of Winter would be a suitable time, given the nature of the Cailleach, but choose a time when the weather and temperature will allow the ritual to take place. If using a beach, check up on when the tide is going out, as it is disappointing to arrive at the beach fully prepared and ready to create a ritual only to find it covered by the sea. Nor do you want to be forced to pack up mid-ritual as the sea encroaches and washes your spiral away.

THE GODDESS

The Cailleach is the "Old Woman," the Goddess who created the mountains by dropping boulders from her apron, and then used them as stepping stones. Scottish mountains carry her name and portray her character. Bein na Caillich (Hill of the Old Woman) above Broadford on the Isle of Skye provides a tough climb with a boulder strewn summit. In Scotland there are many high, rocky mountains amongst which it is rumoured she lives. These include Ben Nevis and the craggy ridge of Ben Cruachan. Myth has it that she carries a hammer in her right hand, and uses it for shaping the hills and mountains as she creates them. Some islands, such as Ailsa Craig, are attributed to her dropped stones.

She is the Goddess of the ancestors, of old age and of Winter. Her place in the wheel of the year is between Samhain and Beltane, the 1st November to the 1st May. Her character is depicted in icy, fearsome winds, and harsh weather, and the Celtic people would call on her for mercy in their bid for survival in the cold climate of Northern Britain. Her association with cruel, freezing conditions may have led to her description as a "blue faced hag."

It is said that Winter starts when the Cailleach washes her plaid in the whirlpool of Corryvreckan on the West Coast of Scotland between Jura and Scarba. She swirls it round and round for three days until the water boils and the thunder can be heard up to twenty miles away. Then she pulls it out, clean and white, and lays it over the mountains to dry. As she does so, Winter arrives, the snow falls on the freezing hills, and the veil of mist is drawn down from the mountain tops obscuring the view.

At the end of the Winter, Cailleach fights the onset of Spring, resulting in turbulent and changeable weather. It is said that when Spring starts she throws her holly staff under a gorse bush and turns herself into a boulder until the end of Autumn. Then she reveals herself once again, and sets about her laundry.

SUBJECT: FORGIVENESS

Holding onto negative feelings harms ourselves more than it harms the unforgiven person. But forgiving someone is harder than it sounds because some of the damage has not healed and some of the damage, we think, is not going to heal.

Forgiveness takes time, as does emotional healing: they are linked and one relies on the other. When forgiveness takes place, healing follows as the canker is removed and the wound cleansed. When the emotions are healed forgiveness takes the place of the hurt. Which first? There is no right answer.

Some people seek holistic therapies and healing; others seek counselling. Reiki can work by healing the emotions allowing forgiveness to be released. To stop the circulation of emotionally toxic thoughts, such as, "I cannot forgive so I cannot heal; I cannot heal, so I cannot forgive," intervention may be needed. Focus on understanding and compassion. Try to envisage the wider picture, focus on the goodness in your own life and let go of blame.

Forgiving yourself is hard. Often we are harsher towards ourselves than we are towards others. There may be an element of embarrassment that fuels disgust at our own behaviour. Now is the time to release this, forgive our self, forgive others and start afresh.

CORRESPONDENCES

THE CRONE

The Crone Goddess is the Goddess of old age, the Grandmother Goddess, who has gained knowledge and transformed it into wisdom. In many societies the Crone, an elder of the community, is revered and respected and her wise knowledge is sought after by younger members of the community. "Croning Ceremonies" are held to celebrate a woman's menopause and entry into the next phase of her life. The Crone is the Goddess of Autumn, the dark months and the descent into Winter.

VEILS

"Caille" is Gaelic for veil, and originates with the Latin word, "pallium." The Cailleach reminds us of all that we hide under our own veils, the veils we pull across the truth that we hide in our hearts. Sometimes our veils may seem like locked doors that we never intend to open. At other times our veils are drawn to hide something from other people. Veils may be drawn when we are not ready to show our true feelings because the time is not right. We may also need to recognise when others draw a veil, leaving us mystified. Sometimes we must pull veils back to reveal the truth, but there are times when we should respect another's privacy and leave the veil in place.

SEA, WATER AND WAVES

The sea, with its element of salt, is cleansing and purifying. Swimming in a clean sea is quite different to bathing in swimming pools or fresh water lakes. There is an element of danger that should be acknowledged, as tides and currents need to be understood, and can pull unwary swimmers out of their depth. However, swimming in safe conditions is an invigorating experience that enables a person to connect with the element of water in a powerful way.

WHIRLPOOLS

The whirlpool of Corryvreckan is known as the "Cauldron of the speckled seas" (*Coirebhreacain*). It is the meeting place of opposing ocean currents that strike a hole in the seabed as well as hitting a subterranean rock pinnacle that shapes the waves of the Sound of Jura into a dramatic vortex. This peaks in strength twice a day as the tides move in and out. The whirlpool is one of the seven largest in the world, and a very dangerous place for sailing.

THE SHORE

The shore is a boundary between the realm of water and the realm of earth, between the physical world and the otherworld, and between mortal earth and the fairy kingdom. Many myths and legends incorporate the shoreline as a place where transformation takes place. The shore is a place that is neither land nor sea, sometimes dry and sometimes under water.

SPIRALS

Examples of spiral rock art can be seen on rock engravings from the Neolithic period throughout Europe, although no-one is sure what the powerful symbol meant to the Stone Age people. There are beautiful rock engravings at the passage burial mounds at Newgrange and Knowth in Ireland, and on Long Meg in Cumbria. Northumberland is the home of many spiral shaped cup and ring marked rocks.

Two spirals are familiar. One is the Archimedian spiral, which continuously moves away from its fixed centre while the distances between the turnings remain constant. The logarithmic, "Spira

Mirabilis," is the spiral found in nautilus shells and fossils such as ammonites, spiral galaxies including the Milky Way, and cyclones that spiral inwards towards the centre. The distances between the turnings increase and the outside opening of the spiral is greater than the inner whorl.

EQUIPMENT

The Altar:
>Symbol for the Goddess: a cauldron of sea water

The Elements:
>Air: a small flag
>Fire: a candle lantern
>Earth: a dish, pebbles and shells

Ritual Items:
>A bucket
>Nine shells
>A white cloth

Libation:
>A picnic in a container that protects it from the sand.

THE RITUAL

This is designed for the sea shore, but can be adapted to take place in the home or garden. Bring the sea shore to your home in the form of pebbles, shells, pearls, sea salt, dried seaweed, driftwood and salt water.

1. Find a place on the beach that is peaceful and unlikely to be interrupted. Create a large spiral on the beach with plenty of room in the middle for you to sit down and meditate, and room for a small altar area. This can be drawn with a stick in the sand,

or made from pebbles or shells depending on the type of beach you choose.

2. The centre of the spiral forms the altar. There is no need for an altar cloth, but you could decorate the spiral centre with beach findings. Place the cauldron of sea water in the centre of the spiral to symbolise the Cailleach and her whirlpool. Fix a small flag to blow in the wind, light the lantern and heap some pebbles in the dish. Water is symbolised by the Cailleach's cauldron. Lay the white cloth and the nine shells next to the cauldron. The picnic remains outside the spiral.

3. Cast the Circle by walking slowly three times round the edge of the spiral. Envisage the protective energy encapsulating the spiral. Include the area in which you have placed your picnic.

4. Call in the Four Directions:

    Face the East: "I call in the Guardians of the East, and the Spirits of the shore birds that inhabit the air and glide on the air currents. Bring your air energy to this ritual. Hail and welcome."

    Face the South: "I call in Guardians of the South, and the Spirits of the fires built by the beachcombers and shore-dwellers. Bring your fire energy to this ritual. Hail and welcome."

    Face the West: "I call in the Guardians of the West, and the Selkies who live between this world and the otherworld, half human and half seal, of shore and sea. Bring your seawater energy to this ritual. Hail and welcome."

    Face the North: "I call in the the Guardians of the North, and the Spirits of the cliffs, dunes and rocks. Bring your earth energy to this ritual. Hail and welcome."

5. Stand at the outside opening of the spiral. Call in the Caileach:

    "I call on The Cailleach, Veiled One, Old Woman. Please be welcome in this spiral. I ask your loving blessing on this ritual. May it be for the highest good of all. Hail and welcome!"

6. State the purpose of the ritual:

"This ritual is to leave behind guilt, confess wrong doing and to restore integrity."

7. Standing at the opening of the spiral, focus on the issue. Take your time. Be aware of the beginning of the spiral as an opening. The energy lies between the lines of the spiral. You walk the energy. As you walk into the spiral analyse the issue in parts. For each part of the issue, stoop and collect a pebble from the beach. Ponder that part of the issue: the pain, the grief, the guilt, the blame. Experience it. This is the last time you will do so. As you do this for each part of the issue, stoop and collect a pebble.

8. At the centre of the spiral it is time to rest. Just BE. Hold the pebbles in your cupped hands and pour your feelings and emotions into them. Allow yourself to feel your feelings and experience your emotions. Then, let them go into the pebbles. Empty yourself out. Name the parts of your pain, shame and guilt and put the pebbles, one by one, into The Cailleach's cauldron.

    Invite The Cailleach to help you deal with the issues. Offer your pain, shame and guilt to the Cailleach and ask her to bring forgiveness and healing. Pick up the white cloth and wash the cloth in the cauldron. Whirl it round and round creating a whirlpool. See yourself being washed clean. Feel the strength of the whirlpool. Meditate on the elemental nature of The Cailleach, the storms, snow, rain, wind, mists and extreme weather that she brings. Stir and stir, scrub and wash. When you feel clean, wring out the cloth and leave it to dry on the sand.

    Open yourself to the sea wind, the sound of the sea, the stretch of the beach, the cliffs and the whole experience of the shoreline. Allow The Cailleach to fill you with forgiveness and the love you need to move on.

9. State the affirmation:

    "I am free of guilt and shame, and restored to full integrity". Take the flag out of the sand, pour the cauldron water over the dish of pebbles and blow out the candle lantern.

10. Pick up your nine shells and without a backward glance walk slowly out of the spiral. Place your nine shells down along the way as an offering to The Cailleach and as a commitment to a new future. Continue the experience of letting go, as the intensity of the centre of the spiral energy dissipates towards the outer rim of the spiral.

11. Give thanks and say farewell to The Cailleach:

    "Cailleach, thank you for being part of this ritual bringing healing to my heart and emotions. Go if you must, stay if you will. Hail and farewell."

12. Give thanks and say farewell to the Spirits of the Four Directions:

    "Guardians of the North, and the Spirits of the cliffs, dunes, and rocks, thank you for coming to this ritual. Go if you must, stay if you will. Hail and farewell."

    "Guardians of the West, and the Selkies of the shore and sea, thank you for coming to this ritual. Go if you must, stay if you will. Hail and farewell."

    "Guardians of the South, and the Spirits of the fires built by the beachcombers and shore-dwellers, thank you for coming to this ritual. Go if you must, stay if you will. Hail and farewell."

    "Guardians of the East, and the Spirits of the shore birds that inhabit the air and glide on air currents, thank you for coming to this ritual. Go if you must, stay if you will. Hail and farewell."

13. Walk round the circle fluffing up the boundary and restoring the space to the physical realm. Leave the spiral to be reclaimed by the sea.

14. Eat the picnic and restore yourself to the physical world. Throw some bread to the sea gulls and pour a little drink into the sea as a libation.

WHAT TO DO NEXT

Habit and self pity tempt us to pick up the pain and guilt, so actively working at keeping the peace with yourself is important. Don't allow yourself to spend time wallowing in the past. Because a ritual has taken place with all sincerity, it has the power to enable you to move forward, and makes moving backwards impossible. Actively creating and taking part in a physical ritual reinforces the fact that a change has taken place. Hold onto that and put plans in place to move forward with your life.

MEDITATION

Close your eyes and relax. Breathe deeply in, allowing the air to be drawn right down to your belly. Then let it go very slowly and gently. Repeat this twice more.

Create a protective bubble of white light around yourself. This is a secure place to which you can return at any time. Hold the image in your mind. You are sitting in the very centre, surrounded by white light. This will not let anything harm you. You are protected and safe.

Sitting in your safe place you feel sand beneath you. Reach down into the sand and pour it through your fingers. Stand up, and find that you are standing on a coastal path, at the edge of the cliffs, here craggy rocks tumble down to the stony beach.

You see a small winding path, and follow it. Although it moves downwards steeply you are able to keep your footing securely. Scramble down the rugged path until you reach the rocky beach.

Stand still, and become aware of the sounds of the shoreline. The tumble of the waves as they crash onto the shore. The screech of the black headed gulls overhead. The cracking of sticks on a fire that is burning sticks and branches amongst the stones on the shore.

Stand by the fire and look into the flames. They leap and spiral in yellow, orange, red and purple. You see all the unwanted things in your life being consumed by fire.

What do you want to put on the fire?

Place it on the fire now.

See it burst into flames, consumed by light, and leaving nothing behind.

Turn from the flames, keeping the warmth of the flames at your back and look out to sea.

You see the tumble of waves, the white horses that gallop amongst the spray, and you walk into the waves. Feel the force of the waves pushing against you. As your swim out strongly the tide gathers you up. You feel the force of the water pulling you along, swirling you out into the ocean. You feel both empowered and at the mercy of the sea.

Feel the drag of the waves and they begin to pull you round in a circle. You are out of control, yet buoyant and exhilarated. The movement gets faster, the current stronger, and you are forced into a spiralling whirlpool dancing in circles with the very essence of life.

Empty yourself out, let everything go, and let the water carry you in one ecstatic whirling dance. Become one with the whirlpool, lost in the rhythm of the gallop of the tumultuous spiral. You are elemental, you are the universe, the sun, the moon, the earth, the sea. All is one.

You are flung towards the shore and carried by a wave to the edge of the water. You rest on the rocks and let gentle water wash over you.

You feel cleansed, purified, refreshed and invigorated.

When you are ready, stand up and walk up the beach.

Find a broad track leading smoothly up the cliff side. As you reach the top of the cliff you walk back into your safe place.

Sit in your safe place.

Breathe in peace, and release

Breathe in joy, and release

Breathe in love, and release

You are ready to open your eyes.

You are back. Welcome home.

Andred

Follow the hare to the dark woods,
Stark silhouette trees, gold-laden skies,
Andred's fiery chariot drives down,
Down to obsidian rivers,
Onyx streams,
Black-mirrored starlight,
See my diamond face.

A face through the water, watching,
Eddies swirl, transforming,
Dark to light, light to dark,
Dark Goddess,
Looking through my eyes.

Unwrap my heart,
Withdraw the thorn that pierces the core,
Sacrificial blood flows,
Atone.

Atone for time gone, time to come,
Time spiralling beyond,
Blood red berries stain my lips,
Drink crystal water
From the deepest well,
Release.

Follow the red deer downstream,
Where oak trees lay their leafy mantle down,
Let the silver sickle moon fade,
I raise my hands to the rising sun.

Ritual for Visiting the Underworld and Facing Fear and Anger

Andred: she of the battle of righteousness, who unleashes anger and rage, and fights unjust wrong doing

Goddess of East Anglia

PURPOSE

To enter the Underworld and face one's deepest fears, recognise and release rage and anger, release guilt and purge one's own darkness.

AIM

To journey into the Underworld, the subconscious. Face fears, acknowledge anger and other negative emotions and memories, and release them.

AFFIRMATION

Though I travel through darkness, I return to the light.

TIME

Winter Solstice, 21st December

THE GODDESS

The Goddess Andred was invoked by Boudicca, the tribal leader of the Iceni, who at the height of her powers in AD60 and AD61, waged her last battle against the Romans. Her husband, Prasutagus, was King of the Iceni under the rule of the Romans, but on his death in AD61 the Romans took over his Kingdom. During the ensuing dispute between the Iceni and the Romans, Boudicca was beaten and her two daughters raped. She retaliated by razing Colchester and London, and then completed the savage rebellion with an onslaught against St Albans. She mercilessly rounded up the Roman women, herded them into the sacred grove near London, and sacrificed them to the Goddess Andred.

The name Andred has been interpreted to mean many things, but most agree that "great", "victorious", "wonderful", "she of the battle", "the invincible", and "she who has not fallen" present an interpretation of her name. Nowadays the French masculine name Andre means "warrior" and the feminine Andrea, means "manly", and "warrior".

During the Anglo Saxon era, Pevensey, an area of Ashdown Forest between Buxted and Ashurst, was called Andredsweald. This was an ancient untamed place, though known well by the gentlemen smugglers of Sussex. The Anglo Saxon word "weald" referred to a wooded area, or forest. Before the Anglo Saxon invasion the area was known as Coed Andred. Other names were Saltus Andred (Anglo Saxon) and Silva Andred (Roman).

Andred was also revered in South East Britain. She has made an appearance in the Eastbourne Lammas Festival, as a mobile giant along with another character from British folklore named Herne. The people of Eastbourne celebrate with Morris Sides, fire dancing and folk music.

One may wonder what we are doing, invoking such a Goddess that accepts such violent behaviour as worship. Boudicca was defending her land, and the land of her people meant survival. Their continuity as a race depended upon the land, and if the Romans took the land, the survival of the Iceni tribe could not continue. She was also defending herself, her family and her daughters from criminal injustice.

In this ritual we will also defend, survive, and regain personal integrity. We will enter our personal "underworld" through the sacred grove. This may unleash very powerful emotions and physical desires. Whilst you "feel" and "experience" the physical side of your emotions and reactions, you do not act on them and play them out in reality if those actions would hurt another person. As we confront our own survival and defence, we ask whether we are justified in our actions, or if there is another way of dealing with the situation.

SUBJECT: RELEASING ANGER

Managing anger is a complex process and the release of anger is an ongoing state, or a series of events, not usually a one-off experience. If you are a naturally angry person, ask yourself if your anger stems from your need to be in control of all the aspects of your life.

Coping continuously with anger can cause blockages in our emotional and mental states of mind and the result may be physical, mental or emotional illness. Presenting a calm mask in front of seething internal turmoil can lead to depression, explosive outbursts, low self esteem, and possibly self harm. By keeping up a pleasant, polite facade, we subdue our sense of self and let those around us remain in oblivious self-centredness. We consider that they are more important than ourselves, or we are afraid to challenge them fearing we may lose them.

Nevertheless, change is needed. It is the manner in which change is asked for that brings success.

Resolving anger is the best way forward. In some cases, however angry a person is, they can talk the situation through, come to agreements, find compromise and release the anger as understanding replaces frustration. Find the cause of the problem, work together to eliminate it, compromise compassionately without being walked all over, and then carry on with forgiveness.

CORRESPONDENCES

WARRIOR WOMEN

During the Iron Age women were not excluded from any area of life, and it was expected that woman would be trained in warfare, and join the men in battle. The concept of Boudicca, Queen, wife and mother, leading a revolt against the Romans would have shocked no-one. Queen Cartimandua was another woman, famous for leading the Brigantes. In mythology we come across Scatlach, Aoife and Medb, Queen of Connaught, all fierce fighting women.

BLACK

Black is not a colour; it is the absence of light. No light waves are reflected back to us, and all light is absorbed. Use black candles, and black crystals, black cloths and clothes.

PURPLE

Purple is a colour of royalty. It brings together the life-affirming survival colour of red for the physical body and blue for the mind and will. Purple strengthens both. For this ritual you need life affirming physicality and mental willpower. Overlay purple cloths, choose purple-red wine or berry juice, and add purple crystals to the altar.

Emotions are important, but in this ritual, do not let your emotions rule. They should not run away with your mind. To return from this ritual, it is your will power that is paramount.

THE HARE

The Hare is a welcome symbol on the altar, and you may want to invoke Hare to guide you through the sacred grove. Renown for breeding and fertility, Hare is born with fur and eyes open, intent on immediate survival. It is said that in that last battle, Boudicca released a hare between her army and the Romans. Hares are symbolic of divination, and may have been considered by Boudicca and the Iceni as a way of divining the outcome of battle.

SYMBOLIC HAND

The printing of the picture of a hand is a later Celtic symbol for the entrance to the Underworld. You may wish to place one on the altar.

EQUIPMENT

The Altar:
> Symbol of the Goddess: black and purple crystals such as black tourmaline, obsidian, hematite and amethyst
> Altar cloths in black and purple
> Tree twigs, branches: use local trees and pick up twigs and branches from the floor
> Fertility: evergreen branches, holly and ivy, pine cones and nuts in shells
> Hand: draw a picture of a hand to represent your intention to enter through the threshold into the Underworld
> Hare: a drawing, statue or photo, to represent your invitation for Hare to guide you during this journey

The Elements:

Air: incense of myrrh and frankincense, or pine and cypress

Fire: a black candle

Water: a dish of water

Earth: a dish of rock salt

Ritual Items:

A copy of The Journey Meditation

Libation:

Dark bread such as rye bread, pumpernickel, fruit cake (Christmas cake), dark gingerbread, dark chocolate

Dark red wine, such as Syrah or Shiraz, Malbec. Heavy "huge" wines

THE RITUAL

1. Set up the altar. Place the words of The Journey by the altar.
2. No candles or symbols are used for the four quarters.
3. Cast the Circle. Imagine a circle of protection that bisects the earth between the "overworld" and the "underworld", containing you in a protective sphere.
4. Call in the Four Directions:

    Face the East: "I call in the Spirit of the East, and the sun of the Spring Equinox. Hail and welcome."

    Face the South: "I call in the Spirit of the South, and the rising sun of the Summer Solstice. Hail and welcome."

    Face the West: "I call in the Spirit of the West, and the sun of the Autumn Equinox. Hail and welcome."

    Face the North: "I call in the Spirit of the North, and the dying sun of the Winter Solstice. Hail and welcome."

5. Sprinkle a very little salt in the water. "I purify this water with the element of earth. I bring earth and water to this ritual. Blessed be."

6. Light the incense. "I bring the element of air to this ritual. Blessed be."

7. Light the black candle. "I bring the element of fire to this ritual. Blessed be."

8. Call in the Goddess Andred: "I call in the Goddess Andred, warrior Goddess of battle, taking the role of the wise hag who accompanies us to the Underworld, to face rage, anger, destruction, and who supports us in our quest for righteousness; please be welcome in this circle. I ask your loving blessing on this ritual. May it be for the highest good of all. Hail and welcome!"

9. State the purpose of the ritual: "This ritual enables me to enter the Underworld and face my deepest fears, recognise and release rage and anger, release guilt and purge my own darkness."

10. Raise energy by walking nine times round the circle chanting:

"Andred, of the sacred grove
In darkness, I seek my foe
And find that foe to be myself.
Face the fear, release the rage,
Look honestly at my naked face
Truth is revealed in this place,
Andred I turn to you."

Feel the energy build up, the expectation of a good result strengthen, and the power of the Goddess become manifest.

11. Settle in front of the altar.

Sit, kneel or stand, but make sure you are comfy. You may want to move position during your journey. Read The Journey, then without the words, experience it. Or tape The Journey and play it to yourself.

The Journey into the Underworld
It is the Winter Solstice.
The sun dies.
It is the death of light.
The earth sleeps.

Andred, the Holy Ancient Goddess leads you to the Underworld.
She is a warrior, a survivor, victorious, she has conquered death
and destruction.
Andred.
It is a time to surrender to darkness.
It is a time to look inward.
It is a time to face fears and take down our self imposed
boundaries.
The Hare runs over the field. It runs towards the woods, the
sacred grove. Follow the Hare. Hare leads you to the edge of
the wood. Here are earth embankments and a deep, dark, water
filled ditch.

Climb over the protective earthworks and jump the ditch
of black water.

Enter the depths of the sacred grove.

The sacred grove is not a place of brilliant light and well
tended trees. It is a dark, untamed place of falling, rotting, giant,
ancient trees. Struggling new shoots force their way upwards,
briars and hawthorn protect the circumference, and creepers
twist and twine on the forest floor. It is hard to penetrate the
tangle of wilderness. You slash and hack. You are determined
to create a path.

It takes courage, stamina, determination, bravery, inner
strength and will power to push through the undergrowth. To
enter the sacred grove and find the threshold to the Underworld
is not easy. Hands are pricked, cut and scraped. A blood-outlined
hand-print is imprinted on the ancient, knarled oak tree. It is
a test and a trial, and only those who are determined succeed.

Those who truly intend to take this journey with all their will, find themselves at the altar.

Here is the place where the dark moon reigns and the Winter sun has retreated behind the trees for the longest night of the year. The earth sleeps, frozen and still, regaining strength, for it trusts in a new dawn, and the return of Spring. Hold onto this knowledge, and be sure that you too will return to the light.

The altar is covered in black and purple cloths. A chalice of blood-red wine stands on it, and the sacrificial offering is your own heart, your soul and your will. Your heart lies bare, your soul uncovered and your will, open and on full view. What will be will be.

The old warrior Goddess, Andred, stands behind the altar. Sense her in the darkness. Now is the time for brutal honesty. The secrets, fears, regrets, anger, rage, horror, destruction, failure, guilt, embarrassment, bondage, addiction, foolishness, the knowledge of evil . . . .

. . . You give these to Andred.

She lays them down on the altar.

One by one.

See them.

Andred can see them.

They lie before you uncovered, stark and grim in the Underworld and in the darkness.

Let out all the raw emotion. No-one judges you in the sacred grove. Let out all the hatred, the anger, the terrifying thoughts, and face with honesty the rights, the wrongs, and let the truth be revealed. Empty yourself. Over and over again, empty yourself.

This is the void.

This is the darkest part of the darkness.

This is the point of release.

The darkness is complete.

The old way is dead.

Desire ends.

This is death.

The cycle is complete.

Andred lights the black candle.

She has cleared the altar of all but your heart, your soul and your will.

The chalice stands next to the candle and glows with otherworldly light.

You discuss with Andred how to correct the balance of rights and wrongs, allow justice, forgiveness, bring equality, and move forwards without the bondage of fear. Listen to ancient wisdom.

Allow her to speak.

She may bring forward ancestors from the Underworld to give you wisdom, or wise spirits to help you, or animal spirits to guide you.

When she has finished she gives you back your heart.

She gives you back your soul.

She gives you back your will.

She passes you the food of regeneration. Eat. Let the food revitalise you.

She passes you the chalice of rebirth. Drink. New life flows to every part of your body.

She gives you the black candle to carry and light your way out of the sacred grove.

As you turn and walk along the path that you, yourself made to enter the grove you hear the first birds sing at daybreak. The sun rises and the first fingers of light filter through the trees.

At the edge of the sacred grove is an enormous ancient oak tree. One faint bloodied handprint is etched on its trunk. You lean against this guardian oak of the sacred grove. Feel its life affirming power, the pulse of energy and its good intention; it feels strong and it fills you from top to bottom.

You can blow out your candle now. The dawn has come. You do not look back. Jump the ditch and climb over the earthwork and walk away. Follow the Hare, forwards, to the light.

12. Take time to ground yourself. Now is the time to eat the bread and cake and drink the red wine, reserving some for Andred. This can be laid outside after closing the circle.

13. Give thanks and say farewell to the Goddess:

"Lady Andred, ancient Goddess of battle, warrior for righteousness, fighter of fear, I thank you for being part of this ritual and bestowing your blessing on my future. Go if you must, stay if you will. Hail and farewell." Put out the black candle.

14. Give thanks and say farewell to the Four Directions.
Move to the North:

"Spirit of the North, the dying sun of the Winter Solstice, go if you must, stay if you will, we trust you will rise again. Hail and farewell."

Move to the West:

"Spirit of the West, the sun of the Autumn Equinox, bringing the balance of dark and light, go if you must, stay if you will. Hail and farewell."

Move to the South:

"Spirit of the South, the rising sun of the Summer Solstice, go if you must, stay if you will, we trust you continue to bring light to the earth. Hail and farewell."

Move to the East:

"Spirit of the East, the sun of the Spring Equinox, bringing the balance of light and dark, go if you must, stay if you will. Hail and farewell."

15. Walk round the circle fluffing up the boundary and restoring the space to the physical realm.

16. Place the libation outside.

WHAT TO DO NEXT

Don't invite your fears back again. Habit dies hard. Stand firm against wallowing in past grief, and know that the grief has been dealt with. Gradually it will fade. You may have to do several rituals to continue to release the grief. Yet at the same time, be aware that by focussing on the grief you may be inscribing it deeper in your psyche. It is a case of using common sense. Sometimes we need to sweep a room several times to clean it thoroughly. Sometimes we continue to sweep by habit, even when there is nothing to sweep. Let go, let go, let go—this is your mantra. Time brings its own healing.

Let go, Darkness
Unchain me
Shake loose your coils
Unbind me.

Release, Dark One
Free me
You cannot, shall not
Keep me.

Awaken in me
Translucent, transcendent
Iridescent Light
I am born
I am
I

Appendix 1

Template for Creating a Ritual

PURPOSE

What do you want to achieve? Decide your purpose, your focus, your intent. Write it down. Be specific.

AIM

What are you going to do to achieve your purpose in the ritual?

AFFIRMATION

Make a statement in the first person stating clearly the outcome. You will align your energy with your affirmation, not state your present position.

Example: "I am healed."

THE GODDESS

Decide which Goddess you are going to call in, who is appropriate to your purpose and intention. What symbols are you going to use to honour the Goddess?

CORRESPONDENCES

What energies support your purpose and aim: time, location, elements, planets, colours, crystals, plants, food.

EQUIPMENT

Gather your implements and tools. Remember matches.

Checkpoint: do the implements and tools for the ritual support the intention or are they surplus to the requirements of the intention?

PREPARATION

Clear the Space.

Take your ritual cleansing bath, or smudge your aura.

Find the four directions using a compass if you want to be exact about the location of each.

Choose which direction your altar will face and set it up in the middle of your space.

Place your ritual implements next to the altar.

Mark the Four Directions and Four Elements by placing a candle or other symbolic object in each of the compass points at the circumference of the circle[8].

---

8   Make sure you leave enough room for moving about during the ritual, without setting your clothes alight.

OPENING THE CIRCLE

State your intention aloud.

Cast the circle. Gather energy within yourself and walk round a circle shape three times. As you do so, point your index and middle finger and intend the energy to flow outwards to draw the circle. Visualise a sphere of white light surrounding you, above and below, bisecting the earth at the point of your drawn circle. Say, "I create this circle of protective white light, a place of protection, a sacred place, between worlds and outside time. I cast this circle three times."

CALL IN THE FOUR DIRECTIONS AND THE FOUR ELEMENTS

Start facing East.

"I call in the Spirit of the Guardian of the East, of Air, the Sunrise, and the Spring. Hail and welcome."

Move to the South.

"I call in the Spirit of the Guardian of the South, of Fire, the Noon, and the Summer. Hail and welcome."

Move to the West.

"I call in the Spirit of the Guardian of the West, of Water, the Setting Sun, and the Autumn. Hail and welcome."

Move to the North.

"I call in the Spirit of the Guardian of the North, of Earth, Midnight, and the Winter. Hail and welcome."

Call in the Goddess.

"I call in the Goddess . . . . Lady of . . . . Please be welcome in this circle. I ask your loving blessing on this ritual. May it be for the highest good of all. Hail and welcome!"

Susie Fox

Raise energy by walking, chanting, singing, dancing, drawing down energy from the moon or sun.

THE RITUAL

This consists of creating or doing something that symbolises the intent and focus of what you want to achieve.

Dedicate the "creation" through the Elements (air, fire, water, earth) by dipping it in the salt, sprinkling it with water, moving it through the incense smoke and moving it through the area above the candle flame.

Dedicate it to the Goddess.

THE "CAKES AND ALE"[9]

This is a time of thanksgiving to the Goddess (and God).

For a solo ritual: take the "Cake," and place a little separately on the plate as a libation for the Goddess (and the God). Say, "May I never hunger." Eat and enjoy. Take the "Wine", and pour a little as a libation for the Goddess (and the God). Say, "May I never thirst." Drink and enjoy. The libation is placed on the earth outside either at this point if you are outdoors, or after closing the circle.

For a group ritual: take the "Cake" and place a little separately on the plate as a libation for the Goddess (and the God). Say, "May you never hunger," and pass to the nearest person. The receiver says, "Blessed Be." He or she then repeats and hands the "cake" to the next person; it is passed round the circle and comes back to the altar. If you are leading the ritual with a second person, each of you will eat before passing it round the circle. Take the "Wine" and pour a little as a libation for the Goddess. Say, "May you never thirst," and pass to the nearest person.

---

9   "Cake" can be bread, or food appropriate to the season, the Goddess, the purpose and intent of the ritual, or the area in which one lives. Ale can be beer, wine, mead, spring water or fruit juice.

The receiver responds, "Blessed Be." He or she then repeats and passes the chalice to the next person; it is passed round the circle and comes back to the altar.

SAYING GOODBYE

The Goddess is thanked and invited to go or stay, but to "fare well" either way:

"Lady . . . . thank you for being here and being part of this ritual. Go if you must, stay if you will, hail and farewell."

Move to the North.

"Spirit of the Guardian of the North, of Earth, of Midnight, and of Winter, thank you for being in this circle and part of this ritual. Go if you must, stay if you will, hail and farewell."

Move to the West.

"Spirit of the Guardian of the West, of Water, the Setting Sun, and the Autumn, thank you for being in this circle and part of this ritual. Go if you must, stay if you will, hail and farewell."

Move to the South.

"Spirit of the Guardian of the South, of Fire, the Noon, and the Summer thank you for being in this circle and part of this ritual. Go if you must, stay if you will, hail and farewell."

Move to the East:

"Spirit of the Guardian of the East, of Air, the Sunrise and the Spring thank you for being in this circle and part of this ritual. Go if you must, stay if you will, hail and farewell."

CLOSURE AND DISBANDING THE CIRCLE

Walk round the circle once anti-clockwise, fluffing the boundary of the circle and bringing the circle perimeter back into the physical world.

Clearing up is very grounding, and a necessary job to be done.

Appendix ii

Prepare your beliefs and pledges for the Ritual with Rigantona

I believe . . .	I believe because . . . (reason)	I pledge to . . .	Who or what does this affect? (accountability)

Susie Fox

Appendix iii

Sun and Moon Water

Prepare for the Ritual with Arnemetia

SUN WATER

A glass bowl
Spring Water
Daylight
Pour the water into the glass bowl.

Place your hands over the bowl. Intend that the sun will energise the water. Let that intention flow through your hands into the water.

Cover the bowl of water with polythene wrap and place outside from morning to late afternoon.

Retrieve before dusk.

MOON WATER

A glass bowl

Spring Water

A full moon

Pour the water into the glass bowl.

Place your hands over the bowl. Intend that the moon will energise the water. Let that intention flow through your hands into the water.

Cover the bowl of water with polythene wrap and place outside under the full moon. Retrieve in the morning.

Bibliography

Anwyl, E. 2006. Celtic Religion in Pre-Christian Times. London: Archibald Constable & Co. Ltd

Chadwick, N. 1970. The Celts. London: Penguin Books

Cunliffe, B. 1999. The Ancient Celts. London: Penguin Books

Davidson, Dr. H. E. 1998. Roles of the Northern Goddess. London: Routledge

Green, M. J. 1977. Dictionary of Celtic Myth and Legend. London: Thames and Hudson Ltd

Green, M. 2003. Wild Witchcraft: A Guide to Natural, Herbal and Earth Magic. London: Thorsons Publishing Group Ltd

Litton, H. 1997. The Celts, An Illustrated History. Dublin 2: Wolfhound Press Ltd

Paine, C. 2004. Sacred Places. (National Trust) London: National Trust Enterprises

Pearson, M. P. 1993/2005 Revised Ed 2005 Bronze Age Britain. London: Batsford Ltd (English Heritage)

Ross, A. 1967. Pagan Celtic Britain London: Routledge & Kegan Paul p. 428

Ross, A. 1967 Pagan Celtic Britain: studies in iconography and tradition. London: Routledge & Kegan Paul

ONLINE ARTICLES AND BOOKS

Birley, E. 1986. "The Deities of Roman Britain," Aufsteig und Niedergang Der Romischen Welt (Rise and Decline of the Roman World. Berlin: Walter de Gruyter http://books.google.co.uk/books?id=24V88LbLUL4C&pg=PA71&lpg=PA71&dq=ratis+goddess&source=web&ots=9jgbQVph_F&sig=aXSa1Q47RUqT7iAPSvYKWzJxuWc&hl=en#v=onepage&q=ratis%20goddess&f=false

Dupe, A.K. 2010. Solstice. Mystical www http://www.mystical-www.co.uk/index.php?option=com_content&view=article&id=82&Itemid=225

Fairgrove, R. 1994. What we don't know about the Ancient Celts. The Pomegranate, Issue 2: Lammas 1997 http://www.conjure.com/whocelts.html

Huathe. 1998. Celtic Festivals. The Sacred Fire http://www.sacredfire.net/festivals.html

Richardson, J. 2010 Magical Powers of Rowan Trees http://joy-r.suite101.com/magical-powers-of-rowan-trees-a245989

Freeman, M. 1996. http://www.chalicecentre.net/celtic_festivals.htm

Furley, R. FSA. 2005. The Early History of Tenterden. Archaeologia Cantiana Volume 14—1992, p 38 http://www.kentarchaeology.org.uk/Research/Pub/ArchCant/Vol.014%20-%201882/04/38.htm

Gyrus, Research on Verbeia http://dreamflesh.com/projects/verbeia/research

Gyrus, The Goddess in Wharfedale http://dreamflesh.com/essays/wharfedalegoddess

Gyrus (Oakley, G.T.) Verbeia, The Goddess of Wharfedale http://dreamflesh.com/projects/verbeia

Kingston, A. & Davies, A. (No Date) The Legend of Boudica http://www.pbs.org/wgbh/masterpiece/warriorqueen/ei_boudica.html

Koch, Dr. John. 2002. University of Wales Centre for Advanced Welsh and Celtic Studies, University of Wales. Lexicon ProtoCeltic-English Word List. http://www.wales.ac.uk/Resources/Documents/Research/CelticLanguages/ProtoCelticEnglishWordlist.pdf

Koch, Dr. John. 2002. University of Wales Centre for Advanced Welsh and Celtic Studies, University of Wales. Lexicon English-ProtoCeltic Word List. http://www.wales.ac.uk/Resources/Documents/Research/CelticLanguages/EnglishProtoCelticWordList.pdf

Morrell, R.W. 1994. Some Notes on St. Anne's Well at Buxton. *Mercian Mysteries No.18* February 1994 http://www.indigogroup.co.uk/edge/Buxton.htm

The Editor 2011. Vaison la Romaine. Travel Writers Coop. Provence-Hideaways. http://www.provence-hideaway.com/208.html All material ©Travel Writers Coop 2011

Wise, C. Elen of the Ways Part 1. http://www.andrewcollins.com/page/articles/elen_1.htm Wise, C. Elen of the Ways Part 2. http://www.andrewcollins.com/page/articles/elen_2.htm

WEBSITES

www.eu.wikipedia.org

http://www.lammasfest.org/giants.html

http://www.peakdistrictinformation.com/features/welldress.php

All material © Cressbrook Multimedia 1997-2008

http://www.peakdistrictinformation.com/features/wellart.php

All material © Cressbrook Multimedia 1997-2008

http://www.colchestertreasurehunting.co.uk/B/bodica.htm

http://www.colchestertreasurehunting.co.uk/C/celts.htm

http://www.roman-britain.org/places/verbeia.htm Roman Britain Organisation

Blessing

Stillness at the centre of the storm
Calm waters under a turbulent sea
Deep love in a whirlwind of emotions
Sun, moon and stars
Light my way
Blessed Be